CLASSIC WARPLANES

NORTH AMERICAN
P-51
MUSTANG

Bill Gunston

GALLERY BOOKS

An Imprint of W. H. Smith Publishers Inc.
112 Madison Avenue
New York City 10016

BESSEMER PUBLIC LIBRARY

J358.4
GunB

A SALAMANDER BOOK

© Salamander Books Ltd. 1990
129/137 York Way,
London N7 9LG,
United Kingdom.

ISBN 0–8317–14026

This edition published in 1990 by Gallery Books, an imprint of W. H. Smith Publishers, Inc., 112 Madison Avenue, New York, New York 10016.

Gallery Books are available for bulk purchase for sales promotions and premium use. For details, write or telephone the Manager of Special Sales, W. H. Smith Publishers, Inc., 112 Madison Avenue, New York, New York 10016. (212) 532-6600

All rights reserved. Except for use in a review, no part of this book may be reproduced, stored in a retrieval system or transmitted in any form or by any means, electronic, mechanical, photocopying, recording or otherwise, without the prior permission of the publisher.

All correspondence concerning the content of this volume should be addressed to Salamander Books Ltd.

This book may not be sold outside the United States of America or Canada.

CREDITS

Editor: Bob Munro
Designers: Oxprint Ltd, England
Color artwork: © Pilot Press Ltd, England
Three-view, side-view and cutaway drawings: © Pilot Press Ltd, England
Filmset: Oxprint Ltd, England; The Old Mill, England; Flairplan Typesetting Ltd, England
Color separation: Graham Curtis Repro, England
Printed in Belgium by Proost International Book Production

AUTHOR

BILL GUNSTON is a former RAF pilot and flying instructor and has become one of the most internationally respected authors and broadcasters on aviation and scientific subjects. He is the author of numerous books, including several for Salamander, including "Modern Air Combat" (with Mike Spick), "The Illustrated Encyclopedia of Aircraft Armament", "Modern Fighting Aircraft", "Fighter Missions" (with Lindsay Peacock) and many of Salamander's successful illustrated guides to aviation subjects. A former technical editor of "Flight International" and technology editor of "Science Journal", Mr. Gunston is an assistant compiler of "Jane's All The World's Aircraft".

CONTENTS

THE North American P-51 Mustang was undoubtedly one of the greatest fighter aircraft of the Second World War. It was one of the few fighters designed after the war had begun which were produced in vast numbers and served on every front. It also happens to have been a very good-looking aeroplane, and, like the Spitfire, it is familiar to almost every aviation enthusiast around the world.

In many parts of the world P-51Ds still exist, many of them in flying condition. They delight crowds at airshows, decorate the jackets of books and appear in countless films and videos. To thousands, perhaps millions, of enthusiasts everywhere, the P-51D is not only the most important Mustang, it is *the* Mustang. Yet when the P-51D appeared, the war was almost over.

At the same time, one has to recognize that by the time the P-51D appeared, in the final year of the war, the rate of manufacture had grown to become a flood, and the D and K models (one made in California, the other in Texas) were far more numerous than all previous versions of the P-51 combined.

It is widely known that the Mustang was designed specifically for Great Britain, though credit for the excellence of the design is due solely to North American Aviation (NAA). The British did not lay down any specific guidelines, and in fact appear to have pretty much let NAA just get on with it. Even in spring 1940, the British Direct Purchasing Commission had over 50 staff based in New York and Washington, and it seems almost beyond belief that at least one engineer, and preferably a team, was never sent to be permanently based at NAA's Inglewood plant in southern California throughout the design and development process.

Had this been done, the Mustang might have been designed around the Rolls-Royce Merlin engine. The machine-guns would

Above: Talk about the Mustang, and most people think only of the P-51D. But as successful and effective as it was, the D represented only one chapter in a long, successful story.

certainly have been of .303-in calibre, and able to take British rimmed ammunition. Not only would the instrument panel have been of standard British configuration, and the pilot's control column had a spade grip with a hand brake lever, but all equipment would have been RAF-compatible from the outset. This is not to suggest that American kit was in any way inferior – though by the summer of 1940 the Royal Air Force's (RAF) combat experience really did count for a lot – but one has only to think of the annoying use of rimless ammunition to see that maybe the British should have taken a closer interest in what the NAA team at Inglewood were creating. And it certainly would have helped if the 1942 production of Packard-built Merlin engines had gone into Mustangs instead of Curtiss P-40s.

It would be ridiculous, however, to give the impression that the story of the Mustang is mainly one of what might have been. From the very start, the outstanding NAA team of designers created what many believe was the best fighter in the world to be flown in 1940, and even one of the best in 1945 when the war ended.

Why was the Mustang so good? Partly because it was designed later than other fighters, and partly because it was designed in California, where there was immediate access to many kinds of new technology. This new technology made the airframe simpler and quicker to make than that of a Spitfire, even though it was somewhat larger. It also enabled this larger airframe to have less drag, so that at low levels – say, up to about 10,000ft (3,050m) – the first Mustangs to reach Britain astonished the RAF evaluation pilots by slipping effortlessly through the sky faster than any Spitfire. Even more remarkable, whilst handling beautifully and being able to overtake a 1941 Spitfire, the newcomer from California had more than twice the fuel capacity of its British counterpart. Later, this capacity was to be considerably augmented.

In 1944, the P-51Ds of the United States Army Air Force (USAAF) played by far the most important role of any fighter in the final elimination of Germany's Luftwaffe

Above: Though a capable aircraft in its own right, the Curtiss P-40 never quite had the "punch" needed to make it an outright winner. The Mustang would soon fill this gap.

from the skies over Europe. That once-proud arm's leader, Field-Marshal Goering, said: "When I saw those Mustangs over Berlin, I knew that the war was lost". Yet at the start of the Second World War, the notion of small, single-seat fighters flying in swarms over Berlin, 600 miles (965km) each way as the crow flies, would have been regarded as ridiculous fantasy.

BUYING ABROAD

Back in 1940, nobody had the slightest idea that such a thing was possible. It all stemmed from the fact that, despite frantic expansion of the British aircraft industry, the RAF and Fleet Air Arm (FAA) were in such desperate need of aircraft that they went shopping in the United States. So did the French, and the US manufacturers, including NAA, were soon overloaded with orders. The Inglewood plant

had been visited as early as 1937 by the British and French, for whom hundreds of two-seat trainers in the NA-16 (Harvard) family had been built. In the last quarter of 1939, the British made the suggestion to NAA that they might manufacture the established Curtiss Hawk 81 fighter under licence, against RAF contracts. This aircraft, powered by the 1,150hp Allison V-1710 liquid-cooled V-12 engine, was in production for the US Army as the P-40,

and was also the subject of big orders for France and Britain.

There was nothing particularly wrong with the P-40, and it was to remain in production in successively improved versions until December 1944. But it was never quite able to take on the top enemy fighters on even terms, at any height, and nearly all the P-40s did their best work in the ground-attack role. NAA management quickly came to the conclusion that their company could design a fighter markedly superior to the P-40, even if they had to use the same engine. They put the idea to the British officials in January 1940. The proposal was not rejected, and after a much more detailed proposal had been made, giving a complete description of the proposed aircraft, the British purchasing commission signed a contract for the prototype, to be known as the NA-73X.

Until quite recent years, the following were thought to be common knowledge: The British commission started out by requesting a substitute for the P-40; in view of NAA's limited experience, it stipulated that the company should buy the

Below: Prior to its work on the new fighter, North American Aviation had built solid but unspectacular types, such as the O-47 (illustrated) and the T-6 two-seat trainer.

History and Development

Above: In complete contrast to its earlier products, North American's NA-73X was sleek and smooth. The aircraft first flew on 24 October 1940, and completed 45 flights.

P-40 wind-tunnel data from Curtiss; that the Mustang was designed by Ed Schmued, a German who had worked for Messerschmitt and so copied the Bf 109; and that because of the serious war situation the British insisted that the NA-73X had to fly within 120 days of the contract being signed. All these are fallacies, and a few more will emerge later.

A FRESH START

NAA did, in fact, pay $56,000 for technical data, mainly aerodynamic, on the Curtiss XP-46, a "next generation" fighter beyond the P-40. Nevertheless, the NA-73X was a completely new design, owing virtually nothing to any other design(s). Despite this, NAA's President, James H. "Dutch" Kindelberger, boasted that NAA could get the NA-73X flying in four months (doubtless the source of the "British time limit" story). Kindelberger was probably the world's most experienced designer of stressed-skin aircraft, and under him were such brilliant men as J. Leland Atwood, who had been chief structures engineer for Douglas; Raymond H. Rice, formerly structures engineer for Martin; and Ed Schmued, who was *not* a

German and had no intention of copying the Bf 109! Moreover, NAA *had* designed an earlier fighter, the NA-50/NA-68, but this was little more than a souped-up Harvard.

The NA-73X prototype contract was signed on 23 May 1940. NAA designers had in fact been working on such a fighter since the summer of 1939, and by May 1940 had completed much of the detail design. They then got down to the huge task of actual preparation of technical drawings, tooling and all the many things that needed to be done to enable quantity production. Clearly, the RAF was going to want not one example but hundreds, and NAA agreed at the start to begin deliveries in January 1941, a very tight schedule indeed. But, true to Kindelberger's prediction, the NA-73X emerged from the Inglewood plant after only 102 days (though with no engine and with

wheels from an AT-6 Harvard). Freelance test pilot, Vance Breese, made a very successful first flight on 26 October 1940. After three more flights, during which valuable modifications were made (for example, to the radiator inlet), he handed over to another pilot who forgot to change fuel tanks, resulting in a forced landing which put the vital prototype out of action for several months.

By this time, however, it was clear that the NAA fighter would at least be satisfactory, and the British soon placed an order for no less than 320, all to be delivered by 30 September 1941. They also gave it the name Mustang. NAA rightly believed many more orders would follow, but first they had to obtain the permission of the US Army for the Inglewood plant facilities to be thus committed. Permission was granted, along with the request that two examples of the NA-73 should be made available, at no charge, for USAAF testing.

The NA-73X's structure was all-metal stressed-skin, the wing having a sheet-web main spar and an almost equally strong rear spar to carry the ailerons and flaps. The use of the rear spar for this purpose typified a design in which many items served more than one purpose; nothing was curved if it could be straight, and overall the

Below: Despite initial disinterest, the USAAC (later USAAF) acquired the fourth and tenth Mustang Is and redesignated them XP-51s for its own flight test programme.

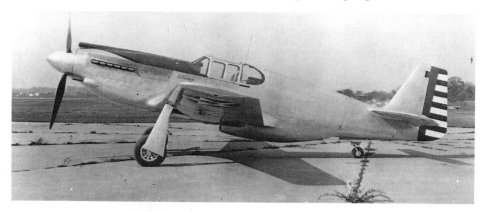

structure was brilliantly simple and ideal for rapid, low-cost production. Moreover, the two spars had to be far enough apart to accommodate the length of a Browning 0.5in gun, only the barrel of which would project ahead of the front spar. Whereas most previous NAA aircraft had left and right wings bolted to a horizontal centre section, the NA-73 was designed with the wings meeting on the centreline, with dihedral emanating from that line.

One of the boldest decisions was to use still very new research by the National Advisory Committee for Aeronautics (NACA), and adopt a so-called laminar-flow profile for the wing. The term was a misnomer. What it meant was an aerofoil whose thickness kept on increasing far beyond the usual location, say to 50 per cent chord instead of about 20 per cent. These new profiles also tended to have little camber, the undersurface being almost a mirror-image of the upper. As the air had to keep accelerating across the wing to a point much further aft than normal, the favourable pressure gradient did tend to keep the flow more laminar than turbulent. In any case, drag measures showed that the new wings were much more "slippery" than the old profiles, and just the thing for a high-speed aircraft. The only real penalty was

Below: A crucial factor in the success of the Mustang was the use of a laminar-flow wing profile. Noticeable in this view is the wing's marked dihedral.

that they were less good at low speeds, so the NA-73X had to have large and powerful flaps. Unquestionably, the best would have been the Fowler-type flap, but for a tough front-line aircraft NAA preferred the simpler slotted type. Wing area was 233sq ft (21.65m^2), compared with 242sq ft (22.50m^2) for the Spitfire, and the NAA fighter was clearly going to be heavier because of its greater internal fuel capacity.

LANDING GEAR

In the 1930s, there had been much debate in the United States over the relative merits of electric or hydraulic actuation for such items as landing gear and flaps. By 1940, hydraulics were beginning to be favoured, and such a system was chosen for the NA-73X. As in the Harvard trainers, the main landing gears were arranged to retract inwards, the large wheels requiring a kink in the wing leading-edge to give extra chord at the root. The retracted wheels were covered by doors hinged near the aircraft centreline, these being closed by their own jacks when the landing gear was lowered. For minimum drag, the tailwheel also retracted.

NAA never seriously considered any engine other than the Allison V-1710. Compared with the Rolls-Royce Merlin, it was a little bigger, slightly lighter and, at low levels and on similar grade fuels, roughly equal in power. But if one plotted power against altitude, the V-1710 performed badly above 13,000ft (3,965m)

Above: To accommodate the large main undercarriage wheels when retracted, a kink was built into the leading-edge root of each wing.

unless (as in the Lockheed P-38) it was fitted with a turbo-supercharger. NAA looked carefully at fitting a turbo, and decided against it partly on grounds of the tight timescale. So the NA-73X had a regular F3R engine, driving a 10ft 6in (3.22m) Curtiss Electric three-blade propeller. The mounting was unusual, but by no means unique. Schmued was naturally aware of the German practice of carrying big liquid-cooled engines on side beams forged in Elektron magnesium alloy, whereas almost everyone else rested them on a complex cradle of welded steel tubes. Lacking huge presses for forging Elektron, NAA elected to use beams made from sheet webs riveted to upper and lower booms exactly like a wing spar. The engine itself rested in rubber blocks.

Whereas the Spitfire had a fuel capacity of 100.8 US gals (381.5 litres), the NAA fighter was given a tank of 90 US gals (340.6 litres) in each inner wing, between the spars. NAA had studied the war in Europe, and from the start gave their fighter self-sealing tanks, as well as cockpit armour and a bulletproof windscreen.

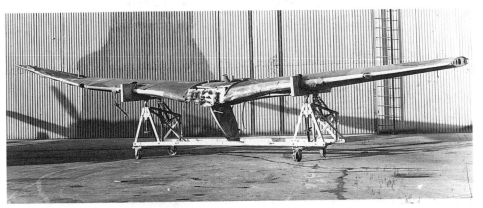

BESSEMER PUBLIC LIBRARY

9

History and Development

Above: An early design modification saw the original carburettor intake extended forward to lie flush with the rear of the three-bladed Curtiss Electric propeller spinner.

The Allison engine had a downdraught carburettor, so the ram inlet was above the cowling. As for the radiators for cooling the ethylene glycol and lubricating oil, this was the subject of much thought – but the thinking was mostly done back in 1939. By 1940, before even speaking to the British, NAA had decided to combine both radiators in a single heat-exchanger matrix installed under the rear fuselage in a duct profiled to give the lowest drag. The only real drawback to an aft radiator is, of course, the extra weight and combat vulnerability of the long pipes to and from the engine. From the start the radiator matrix was a large circular drum, the oil cooler being located in the centre. Prolonged experimentation was necessary to achieve the optimum form of duct and controllable flaps, there being three changes prior to the start of full-scale Mustang production in 1941, three more changes thereafter, and even more sweeping changes in subsequent versions of the

aircraft. By the time the NA-73 was cleared for production, the duct had had its inlet moved down so that the upper lip was lower than the underside of the wing, thus avoiding the ingestion of turbulent boundary layer. Both the inlet and exit ducts incorporated large underside flaps, driven through push/pull rods and bell-cranks from a pilot-controlled hydraulic jack (alongside the flap jack) aft of the cockpit in order to adjust duct area and profile (wide-open on the ground, closed up for high-speed flight). Later radiator designs could even, when closed up, act as a low-temperature ramjet and give positive thrust, but this was not an original design objective.

FIREPOWER

NAA had several good armament specialists, and all were well aware of the need for something better than the traditional "one .30 and one .50" above the cowling. The scheme finally adopted was not only powerful but extremely unusual. On each side of the engine crankcase, canted over almost on their sides, were two synchronized Browning 0.5in guns, each attached to the airframe in a way that did not interfere with quick engine changes. These guns

were staggered so that their magazines could nestle one behind the other in the underside of the nose. Out in the wings were two more "fifties", outboard of which were pairs of Browning 0.3in calibre guns. The middle gun of the three (the inboard 0.3) was mounted at a lower level, so that the forward end of its blast tube was well below the wing leading-edge. All magazines were outboard of the guns, that for the 0.5 being in front, and all three fed through long conveyor chutes located above the guns.

On paper, the armament was outstanding. Like the Spitfire and Hurricane the NA-73 was an eight-gun fighter, but half those guns were of approximately three times the British firepower, besides having much greater effective range and the ability to fire explosive rounds. But there were problems. In practice, these were never fully resolved, though some were of a type experienced by all fighters. For example, in freezing temperatures – which later Mustang versions were to

Below: The wing-mounted armament of the Mustang I was augmented by the fitting of two .50in machine guns, these being mounted low down at the sides of the engine crankcase.

Above: Ammunition belts for the wing guns on this Mustang I are fed into their boxes. Conveyor chutes would feed rounds to the guns when fired.

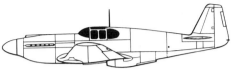

Above: The original configuration of the NA-73X, showing the deep under-fuselage radiator intake.

Above: The Mustang IA incorporated an extended radiator intake and lengthened carburettor scoop.

The ailerons had metal skin and inset hinges, and were driven by cranks at their inboard ends, rotated by pulleys. Each aileron carried a trim tab driven by an irreversible screwjack, again rotated by a pulley. All tail control surfaces were fabric-covered, had inset hinges and neat mass balances recessed into the fixed surface upstream. Again, each surface carried a screw-driven trim tab.

FORWARD SETTING

As might be expected, the header tank for the ethylene glycol cooling system was in front of the engine, above the reduction gear, while the oil tank was behind the engine, immediately under the top decking ahead of the firewall. Behind the firewall, in front of the instrument panel, was the hydraulic header tank. Two landing lights were installed, one in each outer wing leading-edge. Even further out on the left wing was the camera gun. Later, in USAAF versions, this was to be repositioned in the underside of the nose, just behind the spinner. A rigid mast was provided for the radio, which in those days was High Frequency (HF) only. The RAF Mustangs had a British radio which, like the gunsight, was fitted in England.

encounter at high altitude on every trip – various items, such as the firing solenoid and even the gun bolt, would freeze solid. More specifically, a fault of the Mustang was the difficulty of feeding ammunition to several of the guns, mainly because of the sharp curvature of the belt as it reached the gun. Firing at the ground butts was no problem, but pulling hard manoeuvres in combat invariably caused some belts either to jam or to come apart because of broken links. Another long-term problem was stoppages caused by cases and links becoming jammed in the exit chute downstream of the gun.

Another feature not universally liked was the canopy. The cockpit itself was capacious, comfortable and – apart from the arrangement of instruments, which to a British pilot appeared haphazard – well laid out. Unlike several other fighters, such as the Bell P-39 Airacobra and most of the British types, the cockpit heater did exactly what the pilot required. There was also an effective fresh-air system, which took in ram-air from the top of the radiator duct and sucked out the stale air into the same duct downstream of the radiator. The seat was comfortable and suspended

on springs, and the entire back area was protected by armour, mainly 0.3in (8mm). The only real cause for complaint, and then not from everyone, was the canopy. Like that of the Bf 109, it did not slide but was hinged, the left panel opening out and down to the left and the rest of the canopy being hinged over to the right. Such a canopy cannot be opened in flight, though there was a sliding window on each side and the whole assembly could be jettisoned. Moreover, rear vision was not all that it might have been.

The flight control system followed the latest practice, and gave little trouble.

Below: A pleasing study of the first Mustang I (AG345) for the RAF, which took to the air on its maiden flight on 23 April 1941. This aircraft was kept in the US for ongoing testing.

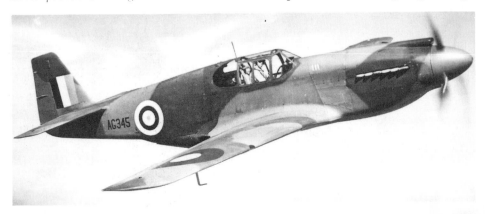

A S noted earlier, Mustang production was launched by an order for 320 placed by the British Direct Purchasing Commission in August 1940. These were to be the only NA-73s built.

The British designation was North American Mustang I, and in December 1940, a further 300 examples were ordered. These were essentially identical, but were designated as NA-83s.

The first of the 320 Mustang Is for Britain was retained by NAA as a development aircraft. It was initially unpainted, though it had a coloured rudder on which the serial was painted by hand (not stencilled). The serial was repeated, much larger, below the left wing and on the upper surface of the right wing. This aircraft did not fly until 16 April 1941, well behind the original schedule, but thereafter it flew intensively in the elimination of problems. The most obvious modification was to extend the carburettor inlet right up to the nose to give good ram recovery at all angles of attack (AoA). Later, after NAA had received a full set of documentation on RAF markings, the aircraft was camouflaged and brought up to standard as a pattern aircraft for exterior painting, but it remained at Inglewood and did not receive guns.

Above: While the first Mustang I remained in the United States, the second example was shipped to the United Kingdom. She was soon to make a big impact on the RAF.

Armament was fitted to the second aircraft off the production line, which was the last to be built with the short carburettor duct. After being brought right up to Mustang I standard, apart from the fitment of radio, gunsight and other British items, it was shipped to Liverpool, England, and first flown from the local airport on 24 October 1941. Next day, it went to the Aeroplane & Armament Experimental Establishment (A&AEE) at Bos-

combe Down, where all missing items were installed. It was evaluated here and at the Air Fighting Development Unit (AFDU) at RAF Duxford. As expected, it proved to be, to quote one famed test pilot, "By far the best fighter ever to come out of America." Maximum speed was found to be 382mph (614.6km/h) at 13,000ft (3,965m). In this respect, it was above average.

In the RAF's opinion, the Mustang I was a super aeroplane up to 15,000ft (4,575m), from 25 to 45mph (40 to 72km) faster than a Spitfire V, with heavy and effective armament, superb handling and more than double the range of any RAF single-engined fighter. The problem was the rapid deterioration in performance at higher altitudes. Amazingly, though doubtless the advantage of replacing the Allison V-1710 with a Rolls-Royce Merlin must have been discussed, nothing was done. Instead, the decision was taken to use the Mustang for low-level tactical reconnaissance, with ground-attack as a secondary mission.

Left: A fine study of a fully operational Mustang I assigned to No.400 (Canadian) Squadron, RAF. Clearly visible are the apertures in the wing housing machine-guns.

North American P-51 Mustang

Left: Visible behind the cockpit of this No.2 Sqn, RAF, Mustang I is the F24 oblique camera and its cover glazing panel. Low-level recce tasks were a speciality.

Most of the first 20 RAF aircraft were retained for special measurements and trial installations. During winter 1941–42, one report noted that the Mustang, with a track of just under 12ft (3.66m) handled better on rough fields or in snow than any other fighter tested. Another aircraft was kept in the air for just under five hours on internal fuel only, and it was shown that even inexperienced pilots could count on a range at medium altitudes of 1,000 miles (1,609km). Accordingly, an F24 reconnaissance camera was installed immediately behind the pilot's head armour, looking obliquely out to the left and to the rear through the existing Plexiglas window. The radio was the usual bulky TR.9D, with a wire antenna joining the mast and fin. As noted, a single camera gun was added near to the left wing-tip.

There was much concern over possible confusion between the Mustang and the Bf 109, and for over a year, through 1942, many of the Mustang Is in front-line RAF service had bright yellow bands painted across the wings.

Initial squadron deliveries were made to No. 26 Sqn at Gatwick in January 1942, and most of the first 320 went to Army Co-operation Command (ACC), usually replacing the Curtiss P-40 Tomahawk or Westland Lysander. Flying Officer (F/O) G.N.Dawson of 26 Sqn undertook the first Mustang combat mission on 10 May 1942, strafing hangars at Berck sur Mer and shooting up a train. The Mustang's reputation had preceded it, and it was a

Below: In addition to the oblique camera, a second unit was carried for vertical coverage, its aperture being located in the lower fuselage behind the radiator scoop. Here, the camera is carefully removed.

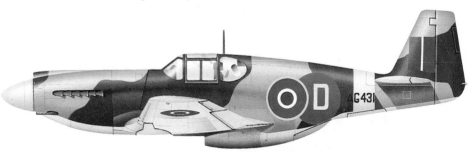

Above: Early RAF Mustangs wore a dark earth and dark green colour scheme. This No.613 Sqn example was used to effect on "Rhubarbs": low-level fighter sweeps hoping to draw Luftwaffe fighters into battle.

Above: A grey/green camouflage was soon adorning RAF Mustangs, as shown by this No.16 Sqn aircraft which flew as part of Army Co-operation Command. Note the repositioned RAF roundel on the fuselage.

Early Service

success from the start. Of course, to take photographs the pilot had to fly past the target on the right at very low level and start the camera as it flashed past his left wing-tip. During the Dieppe raid on 19 August 1942, four Mustang squadrons, most still in process of conversion, had a very busy day. In the course of it, F/O H.H. Hills shot down on FW 190, the first Mustang "kill". Appropriately, he was an American volunteer in the Royal Canadian Air Force (RCAF), whose home was within a few miles of NAA's Inglewood production plant.

As the Mustang force grew, so did the scope and frequency of its operations over occupied Europe. They gradually became

Below: Pilots of No.400 (RCAF) Sqn, RAF, pose with one of their mounts during a break from hostilities. The port-side .50in machine-gun can clearly be seen.

Above: Ground crew swarm over an RAF Mustang and ready it for another punishing sortie. Note how fuel is being transferred to the wing tanks from individual cannisters.

the pre-eminent exponents of "Rhubarbs", preplanned sorties against specific and agreed ground targets, and "Ranger" missions, in which the Mustangs flew aggressively, looking for targets of opportunity. In October 1942, they became the first RAF fighters to penetrate into Germany, in the first instance with a sortie along the Dortmund-Ems canal. By this time the Mustang equipped Nos. 2, 4, 16, 26, 63, 169, 239, 241, 268 and 613 Squadrons, RAF, as well as Nos. 400, 414 and 430 Squadrons, RCAF, and No. 309 (Polish) Squadron, RAF.

Meanwhile, the fourth and tenth Mustangs had duly been delivered to the US Army for testing at Wright Field. They were unpainted except for national insignia and the black anti-dazzle panel. The Army added serials 1038 and 1039 (41-038/039) on the fin and on each side of the nose, together with the "WRIGHT" arrowhead emblem on the rear fuselage. Much later they were painted olive-drab. Another of the myths is that these aircraft, delivered in May 1941, then just sat on the ground. In fact, the US Army was eager to test them but: it was overloaded with other test programmes; the Mustang was a "foreign" type not built to any US specification; and above all, the P-38, P-39 and Republic P-47 Thunderbolt met all possible requirements, so no additional fighter was wanted, and NAA's production capacity was needed to meet orders for the B-25 Mitchell bomber.

ENTER THE P-51

Despite this, the obvious excellence of the new fighter made an immediate impression on the evaluation pilots. Back in September 1940, the US Army had placed an order for 150 Mustangs for supply to

Britain under the lately-passed Lend-Lease Act. For contractual purposes, these aircraft received the US designation P-51, and the F3R engine received US Army designation V-1710-39. Remarkably, and almost certainly reflecting British preference, the wing armament was changed to four Hispano-Suiza 20mm M-2 cannon, with most of the long barrels projecting ahead of the wing leading-edge. NAA built these aircraft as NA-91s, while the RAF allotted the designation Mustang IA; but as deliveries took place after the Japanese attack at Pearl Harbor, Hawaii, many were repossessed by the USAAF, most retaining RAF camouflage and serial numbers. Of the repossessed, 57 were fitted with two K24 reconnaissance cameras in the fuselage. They were to have been designated F-6A, but in the event they were to be called P-51s. Throughout 1941 the name Apache was bestowed, but this was changed to

Above: Because it looked similar to the Messerschmitt Bf 109, yellow identity bands were applied to the wings of early USAAF P-51s.

Above: The first USAAF unit to be equipped with the P-51 was the 154th Observation Squadron, based in

French Morocco. The unit's first operational sortie was conducted on 10 April 1943 over Tunisia.

Above: One of four F-6As borrowed from the USAAF by No.225 Sqn, RAF, for low-level recce work during the

Tunisian campaign of 1943. The F-6A offered longer range than recce-equipped Spitfires also in service.

Mustang at about the time deliveries started, in mid-1942.

In March 1943, a batch of 35 P-51s were assigned to the 154th Observation Squadron (OS) at Oujda, in French Morocco. This was the first US Mustang unit, flying its first mission – a photographic coverage of Kairouan airfield, Tunisia – on 10 April. Soon afterwards, one of the 154th's aircraft was shot down by American flak, a tragedy to be repeated many times because of poor aircraft recognition. Apart from this hazard, the P-51s did splendidly, as did the cannon-armed examples serving with the RAF.

As noted earlier, RAF Mustang Is and IAs were used for many special tests. One was fitted with an F4R engine, as installed in some P-40s, which gave 1,325hp for take-off. This resulted in a different performance curve, inferior above 14,000ft (4,270m) but significantly faster at lower levels. Another tested a rocket-projectile (RP) installation, with a row of four rockets under each wing on Mk I rails, while others tested the Mk II and various experimental rocket installations. Others

Early Service

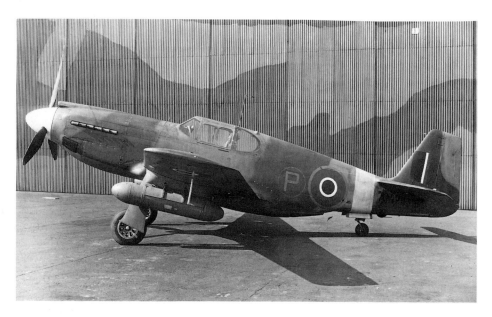

Above: Several RAF Mustangs were to be taken out of front-line service for use as test and evaluation aircraft. This example was used in rocket-firing tests.

were fitted with various marks of the Merlin engine, as noted later.

Partly because of the personal intervention of General H.H. "Hap" Arnold, USAAF Chief of Staff, orders were at last placed for Mustangs for the USAAF. The first order was placed on 16 April 1942

and specified 500 NA-97s, P-51s specially adapted for ground-attack including dive bombing. At first named Invader, they were redesignated as A-36As before the first one flew on 21 September 1942. They differed in many respects from previous Mustangs, notably in having a 1,325hp V-1710-87 engine, hydraulically operated

dive brakes (of the perforated door type) above and below the wings at about mid-chord, a rack under each wing for either a bomb of up to 500lb (227kg) or smoke-curtain equipment, or a jettisonable fuel tank (typically of 75 US gal [284 litre]), and armament of six 0.5in guns, two under the nose and two in each wing. They equipped the 27th and 86th Fighter-Bomber Groups (FBG) in Sicily and Italy, initially sporting an olive-drab and light grey finish, with yellow wing bands and yellow rings round the national insignia. Some reports claim that the A-36A was a failure, with degraded performance and dive brakes that had to be wired shut. This is another myth. Though the speed was naturally reduced by the underwing load, and though casualties in their low-level attacks were sometimes high, the effectiveness of these aircraft in one of the toughest theatres of the Second World War was beyond dispute.

Below: Able to operate from rough-field and makeshift airstrips, the A-36 was a rugged machine. Although primarily a dive bomber, the type claimed 101 enemy aircraft "kills"!

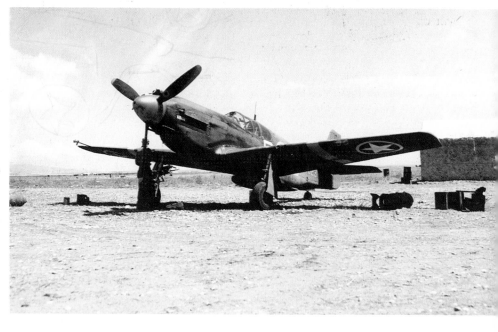

Above: The extended upper and lower wing dive brakes identify this as an A-36 Apache dive bomber. Use of the brakes reduced the aircraft's speed as it initiated its dive.

North American P-51 Mustang

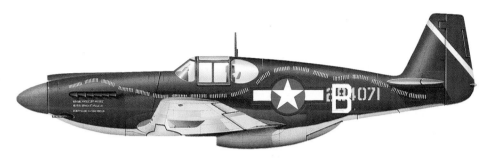

Above: This A-36A Apache served with the 27th FBG, operating from the island of Corsica during July 1944.

The unusual fuselage marking is made up of no less than 190 bomb symbols, representing 190 missions flown.

While the A-36As served primarily in Southern Europe, the majority of the P-51A force was assigned to the

Far East theatre of operations. This example was flown by Col. Philip Cochrane, CO 1st Commando Group.

Next came an order for 310 NA-99s, with Army Air Force (AAF) designation P-51A. These were powered by the V-1710-81 (F20R), rated at 1,200hp for take-off and 1,125hp at 18,000ft (5,490m), or better "upstairs" than the F3R. These aircraft had the same external stores capability as the A-36A, but had no dive brakes and no fuselage guns, the armament being limited to four 0.5in guns in the wings. As before, these guns lay almost on their sides, and many stoppages resulted from the sharp kinks in the belt feed. The first P-15A flew on 3 February 1943, and deliveries began the following month. Of

Right: A trio of A-36As formate for the camera prior to delivery. The Apache force would fly over 23,000 combat missions and drop more than 8,000 tons of bombs during the war.

the 310, 35 were fitted with the twin-K24 camera installation, becoming F-6Bs, some having all guns removed. Another 50 examples went to the RAF, becoming Mustang IIs.

WARTIME ACTION

Thus, by the end of 1943, Mustangs were in action all over the world. Small numbers were sent to the Soviet Union, including ten Mustang Is supplied by the RAF. The P-51s and A-36As served mainly in Europe, especially on the Italian front, while the F-6Bs also served in Europe, mainly with the 107th Tactical Reconnaissance Squadron (TRS) based in England. In contrast, nearly all the P-51As served in the China, Burma, India (CBI) theatre of operations with a large number of FBGs and specialist units, including some in China with the 14th AF. On 25 November 1943, the 530th Fighter-Bomber Squadron (FBS), of the 311th FBG, made the first of the Mustang's long-range escort missions, using drop tanks to accompany B-24s attacking Rangoon, Burma, on a round trip of nearly 900 miles (1,448km).

SEVERAL writers have stated that the problem with the Allison engine was that it had no supercharger. This is, of course, nonsense. Back in 1937, the Curtiss XP-37 had flown with a V-1710 fitted with an exhaust-driven turbo-supercharger, and in 1938 the same maker's XP-40 had been powered by a V-1710 with an integral gear-driven supercharger. NAA discussed the question of a turbo, which of course would have been in addition to the integral gear-driven blower, but decided against it. The result was a fighter which performed extremely well up to the engine's full-throttle height, which varied between 4,400 and 15,400ft (1,342 and 4,697m), depending on the type of V-1710 and the gear ratio of the supercharger. With the V-1710-F20R, a Mustang II reached 409mph (658km/h) at 10,000ft (3,050m). Probably the only aircraft in Britain that could beat that was the Hawker Typhoon prototype powered by a Bristol Centaurus radial engine.

Thus, by the beginning of 1942 the Mustang was recognized in Britain as not only a very good fighter, but aerodynamically the most efficient fighter known. The Royal Aircraft Establishment

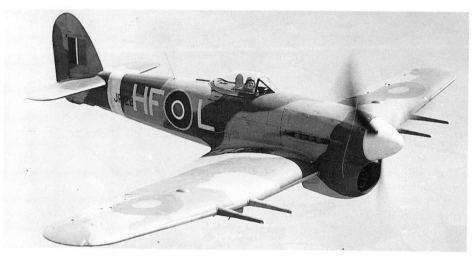

Above: For a fighter-bomber, the big and bold Hawker Typhoon could turn in some impressive performance figures, including a top speed of just over 400mph (644km/h).

Below: Forever associated with the development of Britain's Spitfire, the Rolls-Royce Merlin 12-cylinder liquid-cooled engine would soon be powering the P-51 Mustang.

(RAE) carried out careful tests and calculated the D.100 figure (the drag at an airspeed of 100 ft/sec [30.5 m/sec]) to be 50lb (22.7kg), compared with 65.5lb (29.7kg) for a new Spitfire V. Fitting a Rolls-Royce Merlin engine, which had seemed obvious in 1940, was even yet to depend on sheer chance. The chance could have come at any time from October 1940 onwards. Was it not unbelievable that no US-based British test pilot, such as Christopher Clarkson, was asked to make the trip to Inglewood to fly the NA-73X or any of the subsequent early Mustangs? As it was, it was left to Ronald W. Harker to make it all happen. Ronnie had joined Rolls-Royce as a premium apprentice in 1925, becoming a test car driver, test pilot and experienced military pilot with the Royal Auxiliary Air Force (RAuxAF). On 30 April 1942 he flew a Mustang at the AFDU at RAF Duxford. The rest, as they say, is history.

To say Harker was impressed by the Mustang is to put it mildly. He noted the indicated speed was some 30mph (48km) higher than that of a Spitfire VB at similar power settings. He noted the combat

radius, at least doubled, as well as the rapid rate of roll – a Spitfire weak point, whereas the FW 190 rate of roll was impressive. After landing he said: "It's a natural for one of the new Merlin 60 series." He immediately reported to Hives, and to Ray Dorey, manager of the company's flight test centre at Hucknall. Hives was not a man to mess about; he immediately telephoned Sir Wilfred Freeman, asking for three Mustangs for conversion. Eventually, the company was to convert five.

MERLINS AND GRIFFONS

Rolls-Royce studied various Merlins, including the single-stage Mk XX and the two-stage Mk 61. Considerable work was also done on what was unkindly called "Dorey's Delusion". This was a potentially outstanding Mustang redesigned to have a 2,400hp Griffon 65 amidships, set on a steel-tube cradle above the wing. This was to drive an extension shaft, P-39-style, to a Rotol contraprop and various accessories in the nose, the cockpit being moved right forward well ahead of the wing. Calculation suggested this aircraft would nudge 500mph (804.5km/h), but it was eventually abandoned after a beautiful metal mockup had been carefully studied.

Accordingly, Rolls-Royce pressed ahead with a direct swap, changing the aircraft itself as little as possible. However, there had to be quite a few modifications. The two-stage Merlin was the obvious choice, because of its far better high-altitude performance. The crankshaft was geared to two supercharger blowers in series, giving unprecedented compression of the flow of mixture to the cylinders. So great was the compression that the temperature was increased by 205°C, more than double the boiling point of water. To increase the charge density – and power depends on the mass flow entering the engine – an intercooler was added, requiring an extra radiator. This extracted the heat by the same coolant as used for the engine itself, which in the case of the Merlin was not pure ethylene glycol but 30 per cent glycol and 70 per cent water. After much thought it was decided to put the extra radiator under the nose, in the same duct as the ram inlet for the updraught carburettor, the Allison's inlet above the engine no longer being required.

Rolls-Royce was, and is, one of the few British firms able to move as fast as its foreign rivals. The conversion was authorized on 12 August, the designation

Below: Fitted with the two-stage Merlin 65 engine, this Mustang I displays the distinctive deepened nose and the four-bladed propeller associated with Mustang Xs.

Mustang X being applied. The first Mk X made its initial flight in the hands of Capt. R. T. Shepherd on 13 October. No two Mk Xs were alike, but all had the distinctive deep nose (which was subject to repeated modification), the extra side area eventually being thought to need a small curved dorsal fin. To improve fuel flow at extreme altitudes, the tanks were replaced by metal ones fitted with immersed booster pumps. At first a Spitfire IX propeller was fitted, but from 21 October a larger four-bladed propeller specifically designed for the Mustang was fitted. Altogether, the conversion realized all the improvements in speed, rate of climb and height that had been expected, but in fact it was to be a different Merlin-Mustang that was to go into production. No further aircraft were to be converted in Britain, though the five Mustang Xs were to be kept busy until the end of the war, mostly testing later marks of the Merlin.

FUTURE PLANS

Back in May 1942, Rolls-Royce had immediately informed Major Thomas Hitchcock, US Assistant Military Attaché in London, of their wish to convert Mustangs to have Merlin engines. It so happened that Hitchcock was familiar with the Mustang, and had himself pondered on the advantages of fitting a high-altitude Merlin. He was immediately enthusiastic, and passed the word on to AAF headquarters at Wright Field, and to NAA. The AAF had just received word of a marvellous new Merlin with a two-stage supercharger, and was already talking to the American licensee, Packard Motor Car Co., in Detroit, Michigan, about extending the licence to cover this new family. Fitting it to future NAA Mustangs appeared to fit in well with production plans. There should be no shortage of engines, and V-1710 engines were needed for P-38s and P-40s. Accordingly, a signal was sent to NAA on 25 July 1942 authorizing the conversion of two Mustangs to have Merlin 65 engines sent

Change of Engine

Above: "Peg O' my Heart" displays the new undernose location of the carburettor air scoop adopted from the P-51B onwards. The radiator intake was also reconfigured.

Left: An easy recognition feature of the P-51/-51A and Mustang I/IA was the location atop the engine cowling of a prominent air scoop. Relocation of this item would soon follow.

changed to XP-51B while the work was proceeding. Eventually, the first example was completed and flown, with excellent results, by Bob Chilton on 30 November 1942. The main difference from earlier P-51s lay in the distinctive new nose, with a Hamilton Standard hydromatic propeller with four paddle-type blades of 11ft 2in (3.40m) diameter, the spinner leading into a nose with the dorsal inlet and long duct replaced by a chin inlet immediately behind the propeller. The radiator group was noticeably deeper than before and had a flat vertical inlet. To take full advantage of the expected higher flight performance, NAA restressed the airframe throughout, and strengthened the structure in many places. Another change was to add wing hardpoints for fuel tanks, bombs or other loads weighing up to 1,000lb (454kg) each.

from Rolls-Royce in Derby, England. They were to be designated XP-78.

NAA picked two of the P-51s of the repossessed batch. Both were standard four-cannon aircraft, painted olive drab. NAA, while aware of the need for quick results, could see that this was almost certainly going to be the future Mustang, an aircraft of colossal potential importance. Accordingly, they conducted urgent parametric studies of many possible

engine installations, concentrating on the aerodynamic drag and weight of different locations of intercooler radiator. It was soon evident that the best location was to add it to the radiator group already under the rear fuselage, but exactly how to do this was to take several months and require much tunnel testing, including testing the complete aircraft in the new 40 × 80ft (12 × 24m) tunnel at the NACA Ames Laboratory at Moffett Field, California. The result was very close to an optimized aircraft.

NAA called the conversions NA-101s, so that NA-91-12013 became the first to be completed, and NA-91-12082 the second, the designation XP–78 being

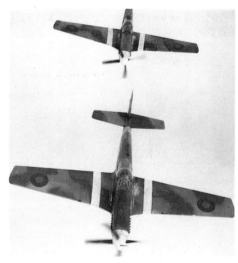

Above: Another distinctive feature adopted by the new generation of Mustangs was a Hamilton Standard four-bladed propeller, as seen on these RAF Mustang IIIs.

Above: Though the aircraft were sorely needed by the USAAF's 8th Air Force to act as fighter escorts to the long-range bombers, early P-51Bs arriving in Europe were to be assigned to the 9th Air Force's 354th FG for use in a more tactical role as fighter bombers.

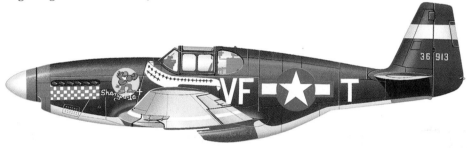

Above: Possibly the most famous of all Mustangs used during the Second World War was "Shangri-La", a P-51B that was the personal mount of Capt. Don Gentile, one of the top-scoring USAAF "aces" of the war. Visible on the white panel are no less than 22 German crosses, each one a "kill".

disbelief and apathetic reasoning to the effect that there was little point in producing airframes without engines, and little point in the planned production of engines if there were no airframes. In fact, Britain never came into the picture at all, though NAA did acknowledge Rolls-Royce's help in solving some of the design problems at the outset. All engines were to be of the Packard V-1650-3 type, based on the Merlin 68, the propeller remained the HamStan and all airframes were made by NAA at Inglewood and at a completely new plant established with great speed at Dallas, Texas. A second factory was needed because of the vast expansion of Mustang production, starting off with a letter contract for 2,200 P-51Bs. Subsequently, this contract was to be modified, partly to take in aircraft already the subject of previous USAAF contracts and partly to take account of new versions.

PRODUCTION CHANGES

One reason for the fact that NAA spent far more man-hours on the modifications than did Rolls-Royce was that the changes were all productionized; in fact, the entire aircraft was gone over with a fine-tooth

The first XP-51B was initially flown without armament, and Chilton quickly established a level speed of 441mph (709.5km/h) at 29,800ft (9,089m). This was well over 100mph (161km/h) faster than the Allison-engined P-51 at this height; even at around 13,000ft (3,965m) the difference was still about 50mph (80.5 km/h), and at all heights the rate of climb was approximately doubled, from just under 2,000 to just under 4,000ft/min (610 to 1,220m/sec). All this time the scene in Britain had been one of political manoeuvring, totally negative argument,

Right: Posing for the camera over a typical rural English landscape, this late-production P-51B sports the black and white D-Day invasion stripes on fuselage and wings.

Change of Engine

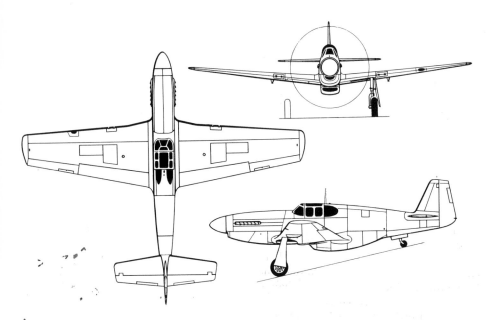

The designation P-78 was changed to P-51B for the aircraft produced at Inglewood, and to P-51C for the almost identical aircraft produced at Dallas. The first P-51B flew on 5 May 1943, and the first P-51C on 5 August of that same year. The total number of P-51Bs built was to reach 1,988.

TEXAS LINE

Dallas built 1,750 P-51Cs. Those on the 1942 and 1943 budgets were designated as NA-103s, totalling 1,350. Aircraft in the 1944 budget were designated NA-111, with minor changes, a total of 400 being produced. An important modification was that the Block-15 P-51Bs, and nearly all Block-10 P-51Cs, had the V-1650-7 engine, with powers generally raised by

Above: The P-51B was the first Mustang Model to be powered by the Packard-built Merlin engine, a change which necessitated some relatively major modifications to the aircraft's lines ahead of the cockpit.

comb to see where changes might usefully be introduced to improve ease of servicing, reduce manufacturing time or enhance performance. As a result, some 90 changes were introduced that had nothing to do with the engine. One was to improve the design of the already excellent ailerons. Not least, the radiator installation was, after many changes, perfected with a visibly different bottom line, a sharply-angled inlet standing more than 2in (5cm) away from the underside of the wing, and a modified matrix and door arrangement. Instead of the oil cooler being in the centre of a circular coolant radiator, it was relocated at the front of the duct with its own ventral exit door. Further downstream, in a greatly enlarged duct, was the huge rectangular coolant matrix, with a much bigger exit door at the rear. Another modification was to standardize on the armament of four 0.5in wing guns only.

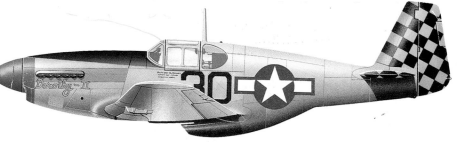

Above: The yellow and black tail checkers identify this P-51Bs unit as the 325th FG, 15th AF, USAAF. The aircraft was used in support of the

Allied campaign in Italy during late-1944. By this time, camouflage paint had all but given way to the natural metal finish illustrated.

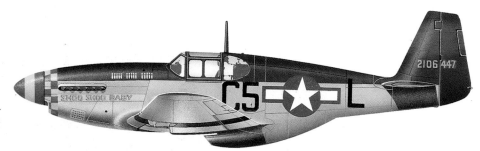

Above: A Block 15 P-51B from the Inglewood production line, "Shoo Shoo Baby" wears a "half and half" colour scheme of olive drab and

natural metal. Stripping the paint off helped reduce drag and boosted the Mustang's airspeed by around 20mph (32km/h).

PRODUCTION

P-51B Production

AAF Serials:

43-12093	– 43-12492
43-6313	– 43-6352
43-6353	– 43-6752
43-6753	– 43-7112
43-7113	– 43-7202
42-106429	– 42-106538
42-106541	– 42-106738
42-106739	– 42-106908
42-106909	– 42-106978
43-24752	– 43-24901

P-51C Production

AAF Serials:

42-102979	– 42-103328
42-103329	– 42-103378
42-103379	– 42-103778
42-103779	– 42-103987
43-24902	– 43-25251
44-10753	– 44-11152

50 to 100hp. A total of 91 aircraft from the Block-10 production (71 P-51B-10-NA and 20 P-51C-10-NT, NT being the code for NAA Texas) were fitted with two oblique K24 cameras, or a K17 and a K22, to become F-6C photographic aircraft. Most, if not all, retained their guns.

Throughout the second half of 1942, the excellence of the Mustang was the subject of intense discussion in London. Even the inevitable doubters were ultimately convinced. In general, the RAF had ceased to have interest in US fighters, but the Mustang was very much the exception. There was considerable fear that all the new Packard-engined aircraft would go to the USAAF, but eventually various deals were worked out in late-1942 which, among other things, involved transfer of Spitfire VBs to the 8th AF in England, mainly for use as fighter-trainers. Thus the way was clear for Lend-Lease supplies to continue of the new models, the RAF receiving 274 P-51Bs and 636 P-51Cs. A

Right: Proof of the Mustang's in-built strength, as the pilot takes a closer look at the damage to the wing caused by a burst of flak.

total of 59 were diverted to the Royal Australian Air Force (RAAF) and other Allied air arms.

Throughout 1942, plans had gone ahead for the US 8th Air Force to be built up in England as a mighty force to attack occupied Europe. To avoid crippling losses escort fighters were needed, and several big and costly new fighters were developed specifically to do this job. There was also the Republic P-47 Thunderbolt which, despite its size and weight, was an excellent all-rounder; but it did not quite have the range, and there was nowhere to put extra fuel except externally. One of the purpose-built escorts was the Fisher XP-75. Colonel (later General) Mark E. Bradley tested the Fisher and decided something else had to be found – and quickly. He called Kindelberger and ordered a P-51B to be fitted

with an extra fuel tank behind the pilot's seat, between the radiator duct and the radios. He knew this would make directional stability almost unacceptable, so that for the first hour or so the pilot would have to concentrate on keeping the nose on the right point on the horizon; after that time the extra tank would be empty. With two drop tanks this would mean a total capacity of 419 US gal (1,586 litre).

NAA quickly installed the extra self-sealing tank. Bradley had the P-51B filled up, complete with drop tanks, and then made a rather protracted take-off. On his first test he flew to Albuquerque, New Mexico, circled the city and flew back. He was rather pleased; he had just done the equivalent of England to Berlin. There was no need to look any further. The extra tank went into the last 550 P-51Bs, becoming Block-7 aircraft, and the

Change of Engine

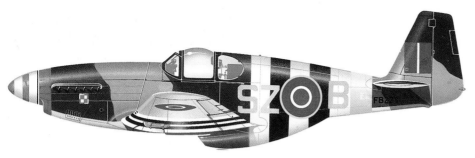

P-51Cs became Block-3 aircraft. The tank was also retrofitted into many aircraft already built. In service, however, the directional instability was judged to be a hazard for inexperienced pilots, and the tank was usually restricted to 65 US gal (245 litre). It still made a crucial difference to combat radius, and was standard on all future production versions.

Above: One of 300 P-51B/Cs supplied to the RAF under the terms of the Lend-Lease agreement with the US (another 20 were lost at sea while on their delivery voyage), this Mustang IIIB served with No.316 (Polish) Squadron during the huge Allied push into Europe on D-Day.

COMBAT DEBUT

The first combat unit with the new Mustang was the 354th Fighter Group (FG), which reached England in October 1943. To the dismay of the 8th AF, this unit was assigned to the tactical 9th AF for ground-attack duties, but a compromise was reached whereby they would help escort the 8th's bombers until further P-51B Groups became available. Thus the 354th flew the first mission on 1 December 1943, and scored the type's first victory on a mission to Bremen in Germany on 16 December; but inexperienced pilots and

Above: No.19 Squadron was the first RAF unit to receive the Mustang III. Though the aircraft were delivered with the original flat-style canopy, the RAF gradually replaced these with the so-called Malcolm hood, which gave an almost all-round view.

Below: An underwing fuel tank is attached to its hardpoint as work continues to prepare this P-51B for a long-range escort mission.

Above: About to receive some much-needed maintenance, this P-51C was a Block-5 production aircraft built on North American's Dallas line.

PRODUCTION

Mustang III Production

RAF Serials:
FB100 – FB399
FR411
FX848 – FX999
FZ100 – FZ197
HB821 – HB961
HK944 – HK947
HK955 – HK956
KH421 – KH640
SR406 – SR438
SR440

ground crews, and numerous technical problems, limited operations with the P-51B and C until about eight weeks into 1944. By that time the strength of Mustang Groups was building up in both the 8th and 9th AFs, and from the early spring of 1944 the improved fighter became a force to be reckoned with.

Meanwhile, the first RAF station to receive Mustang IIIs was Gravesend in Kent, initially equipping No. 65 Sqn in late December 1943, followed by No. 19 Sqn in March 1944. Later, the Mk III equipped not only these but also Nos. 66, 94, 112, 118, 122, 126, 129, 165, 249, 260, 306, 309, 315, 316 and 345 Sqns, and No. 541 Sqn of RAF Coastal Command. After the aircraft for all these units had been built and delivered to England, the RAF

decided that the cockpit canopy was "not acceptable for European operations" – something which, with a few seconds' thought, they could have decided in the summer of 1940, with advantage to all subsequent Mustangs. As it was, a fairly major modification was devised in which the existing hood was replaced by a bulged Perspex canopy sliding to the rear

on rails. It gave the pilot what seemed like twice as much room, and the huge goldfish bowl afforded a good view almost straight down or directly to the rear, though with increasing distortion as the angle increased. This hood, made and fitted by R. Malcolm & Co., was also fitted as a field modification to many USAAF aircraft at British bases.

Above: The sleek body lines of the Mustang are highlighted by the natural metal finish on this, one of the final production Mustang IIIs built for the RAF. No less than 18 RAF squadrons operated this model.

Above: Major John "Pappy" Herbst was the leading USAAF P-51 ace in the Far East, with 17 "kills".

Above: Though the Malcolm hood was a British design, many USAAF P-51s were soon retrofitted with this new canopy as a field modification. This P-51B wears the fuselage codes of the 374th FS, 361st FG.

THE P-51D cured virtually every one of the Mustang's few shortcomings, and it was this version, along with its Texas-built counterpart, the P-51K, that finally defeated the once-proud Luftwaffe, shooting the Swastika-bearing aircraft from the skies and hunting them down in remote hiding places on the ground.

By far the most obvious new feature of the P-51D was the sliding "teardrop" canopy. As emphasized previously, it was the fault of the British that, despite the presence of such experienced RAF test pilots as Christopher Clarkson in offices in New York and Washington, nobody was sent to Inglewood in 1940 to see how the only warplane actually being designed for Britain was shaping up. It seems doubly strange that, having adopted sliding canopies in the Harvard family which could be opened in flight and gave

Below: The sight of P-51Ds (seen here with an older P-51B) flying deep into enemy territory was to become increasingly common as the USAAF bomber raids intensified.

excellent all-round vision, the Mustang should have had a canopy described in a British document of *three years later* as "overall, unacceptable".

It should never have been left for a British company to devise an interim improved hood in 1943, and to fit this to numerous Mustangs as a field modification. Fortunately, by the summer of 1943 something was at last being done to improve Mustangs on the production line. Following discussions with the British, and examination of the clear-blown "teardrop" canopies of later Spitfires and Typhoons, NAA secured agreement to test a similar canopy on a Mustang. The aircraft chosen was one of the first P-51Bs, and it flew with the new hood on 17 November 1943. At first glance one might have thought the huge Plexiglas moulding far larger than necessary, but pilots who flew the aircraft thought it wonderful. The original hood had made the upper part of the cockpit somewhat cramped, especially for tall pilots, but the new pattern – and even bigger patterns were fitted later – could have accommodated a pilot 7ft

(2.1m) tall! It gave almost unobstructed vision around 360deg, with no significant distortion. The large rear section, which did not reach its point of maximum height until well behind the pilot's head, was the shape offering the best combination of viewing angles and minimum aerodynamic drag. To show how much room there was, late in the war at least nine P-51Ds were fitted with a second seat, behind the original one, without modifying the canopy. Possibly the only drawback was that at least half the Mustang pilots needed extra cushions in order to get their eyes level with the gunsight and see over the sill of the giant canopy.

Of course, in order to accommodate the new hood the rear fuselage was cut down, though not by as much as it appeared to be. The necessary modifications to the fuselage tooling were not extensive, and very little restressing of the structure was necessary. The Plexiglas was mounted in rubber in a metal frame, the sill round the bottom being exceptionally deep. This was needed to provide the strength and rigidity required to avoid distortion and

Above: The most obvious external difference on the P-51D/K was the new teardrop Plexiglas canopy. Far better than previous canopies, the new hood offered an all-round view.

the very dangerous binding or jamming in the fuselage rails that could have resulted. There were actually three rails, one along each side of the cockpit and the third along the upper centreline of the rear fuselage. The canopy was opened and closed by a crank handle below the right end of the massive windscreen frame (which was not altered). The handle could be locked in various intermediate positions, but it was not normal to open the canopy in flight, and never at high speed. Late-production Mustangs had even more room in the cockpit, the upper part of the moulding being raised by bulges at the front and rear; this was most obvious at the rear end, and was especially welcome on two-seaters.

Having proved the concept, NAA completed two P-51Bs as XP-51Ds, each with the proposed production version of the canopy and rear fuselage. They also incorporated a further modification that was, if anything, even more important than the new canopy: the wing armament was completely redesigned.

A BIGGER PUNCH

One obvious shortcoming of the P-51B was that it had rather limited firepower. Moreover, the two guns in each wing were installed leaning over at quite sharp angles, and this seriously affected the belt feeds. NAA determined to redesign the installation, and eventually achieved an excellent arrangement of three 0.5in guns in each wing, all upright and fed with unkinked belts. The only insoluble problem was that the belts for the inboard guns had to arch across the middle guns in the trio, but belt jams and feed stoppages were almost unknown. As finally put into production, the inboard guns each had

400 rounds of ammunition, the others each having 270 rounds. Users had the option of removing two guns and having just four, as in the P-51B, with 400 rounds each, and some pilots did select this.

One of the visually obvious modifications was the increase in the root chord of the wing. The main landing gears were strengthened to accept the increased weights of up to 12,100lb (5,493kg), but the tyres remained at 27in (68.5cm) diameter. Despite this, the wheel bays and doors were modified, and the kink in the wing leading-edge made much more pronounced. On the P-51B it was barely perceptible, whereas on the P-51D the change in leading-edge taper was 20deg, giving a better profile at the wing root.

It will be recalled that the addition of the 85 US gal (322.7 litre) tank in the rear

Below: The opportunity was taken to increase the Mustang's firepower on the new model, with an extra pair of machine-guns being added to the wings for a total of six guns.

The P-51 D and K

Above: Caught on its final approach before landing, this P-51D shows the classic lines of NAA's fighter which were essentially retained despite some major structural modifications.

fuselage adversely affected the Mustang's directional stability. The loss of keel area at the rear caused by cutting down the top line of the rear fuselage naturally accentuated this, and early in the production of the P-51D a dorsal fin was added, which also enhanced the aircraft's appearance. This extra fin area was also added as a field modification to some aircraft already delivered. The extra weight, drag and cost were insignificant, yet this quite small additional fin area made a noticeable difference, especially when the rear fuselage fuel tank was full. Conversely, a small number of aircraft were completed with the original canopy and Dash-3 engine, some of these later being re-engined.

By 1944 NAA's Dallas production plant was in full swing, and in that calendar year the two factories together delivered almost 9,000 Mustangs. Discounting the NA-106 rebuilds, Inglewood produced 6,502 P-51Ds, and Dallas 1,454. A total of

Right: Built in greater numbers than all other Mustang variants combined, the P-51D/K was to be supplied in considerable numbers to Britain as the Mustang IV/IVA respectively.

280 went to the RAF as Mustang IVs. Almost all Block-25 and subsequent examples had underwing hardpoints not only for two 1,000lb (454kg) bombs, or fuel tanks, but alternatively for various rocket launchers. The latter included zero-length stubs for six 5in (12.7cm) high-velocity aircraft rockets (HVARs), or as many as ten if no drop tanks were carried; alternatively "Bazooka" tubes of plastic,

steel or magnesium alloy were carried in triple clusters.

The Dallas plant also built 1,500 P-51Ks, which differed from the P-51D only in having an Aeroproducts propeller. Though this had a diameter of 11ft (3.35m), performance was indistinguishable. As with the P-51D, stubs for rockets were introduced at Block-10. No fewer than 594 P-51Ks went under Lend-Lease to the RAF, these receiving the Mustang IVA designation.

More than 20 of the Dallas-built P-51Ds became TP-51D conversion trainers, ten aircraft being completed to this standard, the rest being converted. The ten aircraft built had the modified canopy, as described earlier, and dual flight controls, though the backseater did not have a complete duplicate set of instruments and other

Below: Along with an increase in the wing armament, the underwing hardpoints were beefed up to allow a wider range of weapons, such as these "Bazooka" rocket units, to be carried.

Above: The Dallas-built P-51Ks were virtually indistinguishable from the Inglewood-built P-51Ds, but they did introduce a redesigned canopy and an Aeroproducts propeller.

control interfaces. Most of the conversions retained the original canopy. There were also unofficial two-seat conversions, including even a P-51B rebuilt with a side-facing rear seat and hinged rear canopy by the 335th FS of the top-scoring 4th FG at Debden, England. Even more remarkably, there were at least three instances of two pilots riding in standard P-51Ds: Lt. Royce Priest, Lt. George D.

PRODUCTION

F-6D Production

AAF Serials:
44-13020 – 44-13039
44-13131 – 44-13140
44-13181
44-84059 – 44-84540
44-84566
44-84773 – 44-84788
44-84835 – 44-84855
45-11655 – 45-11689

This model was later redesignated FP-51D and RF-51D.

F-6K Production

AAF Serials:
44-11554
44-11897 – 44-11952
44-11993 – 44-12008
44-12216 – 44-12237
44-12459 – 44-12471
44-12523 – 44-12534
44-12810 – 44-12852

This model was later redesignated FP-51K and RF-51K.

Green and Sqn. Ldr. Eugeniusz Horbaczewski, all of whom landed beside comrades shot down in hostile territory and brought them back, flying the aircraft whilst sitting on the lap of the rescuee.

CAMERA SHIPS

A total of 163 P-51K-5 to -15s were completed as F-6K photo-reconnaissance aircraft, and 136 P-51D-NAs from Blocks -20, -25 and -30 were converted after completion as F-6Ds, with further small numbers being converted around the end of the war. All these photographic aircraft were basically similar: two cameras, usually a K17 and a K22, were installed in the rear fuselage, one looking almost horizontally out to the left and the other below it at an oblique angle. The camera bay was nowhere near where it had been in previous F-6 versions, being just ahead of the tailwheel compartment. A further modification of most F-6Ds and Ks was to fit a direction finding (D/F) receiver, served by a rotating loop antenna behind the main HF mast just in front of the dorsal fin. So far as is known, all F-6D/K aircraft retained their armament. Certainly this

Below: The two camera ports located towards the rear of the fuselage identify this as an F-6D photo-ship. The third (vertical) camera can just be seen on the rear underfuselage.

was the case with two aircraft from the 82nd TRS on a mission over the Philippines on 11 January 1945. They encountered a Mitsubishi G4M bomber escorted by 12 Japanese fighters; Capt. Shomo shot down six of the fighters, and his wingman, Lt. Lipscombe, claimed three. Shomo, an embalmer in peacetime, had aptly named his photo-ship *The Flying Undertaker*.

Of course, a fighter's effectiveness depends crucially upon how accurately the pilot can shoot. In the P-51B/C the standard gunsight was the N-3B, a simple reflector sight with no controls except a rheostat to make the aiming "pipper" brighter or dimmer. The pilot needed plenty of skill to judge the aim-off deflection needed, and then manoeuvre the aircraft to point the desired degree ahead of the enemy's direction of travel (which could be in almost any direction). The P-51B/C were also the first USAAF versions to have a camera gun fitted as standard, the 0.6in (16mm) N-1 being installed at the extreme root of the left wing. All too often, the film showed why the firing bursts had missed the target. With the P-51D/K the gunsight was improved to the N-9, this featuring a larger aiming ring with the pipper in the centre. Then came the miracle sight from England (or rather Scotland). Drawings of the RAF gyro gunsight (GGS) were supplied to the USAAF, and it was put into production as the K-14, going on to the P-51D line ahead of all other aircraft

The P-51 D and K

North American P-51D Mustang cutaway drawing key

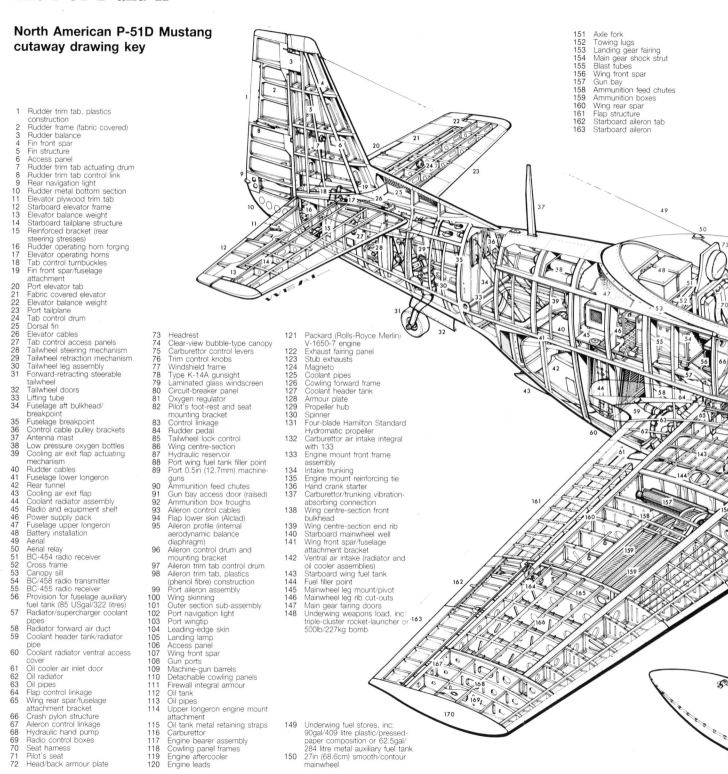

1 Rudder trim tab, plastics construction
2 Rudder frame (fabric covered)
3 Rudder balance
4 Fin front spar
5 Fin structure
6 Access panel
7 Rudder trim tab actuating drum
8 Rudder trim tab control link
9 Rear navigation light
10 Rudder metal bottom section
11 Elevator plywood trim tab
12 Starboard elevator frame
13 Elevator balance weight
14 Starboard tailplane structure
15 Reinforced bracket (rear steering stresses)
16 Rudder operating horn forging
17 Elevator operating horns
18 Tab control turnbuckles
19 Fin front spar/fuselage attachment
20 Port elevator tab
21 Fabric covered elevator
22 Elevator balance weight
23 Port tailplane
24 Tab control drum
25 Dorsal fin
26 Elevator cables
27 Tab control access panels
28 Tailwheel steering mechanism
29 Tailwheel retraction mechanism
30 Tailwheel leg assembly
31 Forward-retracting steerable tailwheel
32 Tailwheel doors
33 Lifting tube
34 Fuselage aft bulkhead/breakpoint
35 Fuselage breakpoint
36 Control cable pulley brackets
37 Antenna mast
38 Low pressure oxygen bottles
39 Cooling air exit flap actuating mechanism
40 Rudder cables
41 Fuselage lower longeron
42 Rear tunnel
43 Cooling air exit flap
44 Coolant radiator assembly
45 Radio and equipment shelf
46 Power supply pack
47 Fuselage upper longeron
48 Battery installation
49 Aerial
50 Aerial relay
51 BC-454 radio receiver
52 Cross frame
53 Canopy sill
54 BC-458 radio transmitter
55 BC-455 radio receiver
56 Provision for fuselage auxiliary fuel tank (85 USgal/322 litres)
57 Radiator/supercharger coolant pipes
58 Radiator forward air duct
59 Coolant header tank/radiator pipe
60 Coolant radiator ventral access cover
61 Oil cooler air inlet door
62 Oil radiator
63 Oil pipes
64 Flap control linkage
65 Wing rear spar/fuselage attachment bracket
66 Crash pylon structure
67 Aileron control linkage
68 Hydraulic hand pump
69 Radio control boxes
70 Seat harness
71 Pilot's seat
72 Head/back armour plate

73 Headrest
74 Clear-view bubble-type canopy
75 Carburettor control levers
76 Trim control knobs
77 Windshield frame
78 Type K-14A gunsight
79 Laminated glass windscreen
80 Circuit-breaker panel
81 Oxygen regulator
82 Pilot's foot-rest and seat mounting bracket
83 Control linkage
84 Rudder pedal
85 Tailwheel lock control
86 Wing centre-section
87 Hydraulic reservoir
88 Port wing fuel tank filler point
89 Port 0.5in (12.7mm) machine-guns
90 Ammunition feed chutes
91 Gun bay access door (raised)
92 Ammunition box troughs
93 Aileron control cables
94 Flap lower skin (Alclad)
95 Aileron profile (internal aerodynamic balance diaphragm)
96 Aileron control drum and mounting bracket
97 Aileron trim tab control drum
98 Aileron trim tab, plastics (phenol fibre) construction
99 Port aileron assembly
100 Wing skinning
101 Outer section sub-assembly
102 Port navigation light
103 Port wingtip
104 Leading-edge skin
105 Landing lamp
106 Access panel
107 Wing front spar
108 Gun ports
109 Machine-gun barrels
110 Detachable cowling panels
111 Firewall integral armour
112 Oil tank
113 Oil pipes
114 Upper longeron engine mount attachment
115 Oil tank metal retaining straps
116 Carburettor
117 Engine bearer assembly
118 Cowling panel frames
119 Engine aftercooler
120 Engine leads

121 Packard (Rolls-Royce Merlin) V-1650-7 engine
122 Exhaust fairing panel
123 Stub exhausts
124 Magneto
125 Coolant pipes
126 Cowling forward frame
127 Coolant header tank
128 Armour plate
129 Propeller hub
130 Spinner
131 Four-blade Hamilton Standard Hydromatic propeller
132 Carburettor air intake integral with 133
133 Engine mount front frame assembly
134 Intake trunking
135 Engine mount reinforcing tie
136 Hand crank starter
137 Carburettor/trunking vibration-absorbing connection
138 Wing centre-section front bulkhead
139 Wing centre-section end rib
140 Starboard mainwheel well
141 Wing front spar/fuselage attachment bracket
142 Ventral air intake (radiator and oil cooler assemblies)
143 Starboard wing fuel tank
144 Fuel filler point
145 Mainwheel leg mount/pivot
146 Mainwheel leg rib cut-outs
147 Main gear fairing doors
148 Underwing weapons load, inc: triple-cluster rocket-launcher or 500lb/227kg bomb

149 Underwing fuel stores, inc: 90gal/409 litre plastic/pressed-paper composition or 62.5gal/284 litre metal auxiliary fuel tank
150 27in (68.6cm) smooth/contour mainwheel

151 Axle fork
152 Towing lugs
153 Landing gear fairing
154 Main gear shock strut
155 Blast tubes
156 Wing front spar
157 Gun bay
158 Ammunition feed chutes
159 Ammunition boxes
160 Wing rear spar
161 Flap structure
162 Starboard aileron tab
163 Starboard aileron

164 Starboard aileron tab
    adjustment mechanism (ground
    setting)
165 Wing rib strengthening
166 Outboard section structure
167 Outer section single spar
168 Wingtip sub-assembly
169 Starboard navigation light
170 Detachable wingtip

(the Dallas-built P-51K followed some time later). The K-14 merely required the pilot to know the wingspan of the enemy aircraft, which he then dialled into the sight (indeed, at the end of the war the dial was actually marked with the principal Luftwaffe types, thus avoiding the need for any thought at all). Next, the pilot fed in the target range by turning a handgrip projecting horizontally from the top of the throttle lever. Adjusting the range varied the diameter of a ring formed by six bright diamond shapes. All the pilot had to do then was get the target wingtips on the bright ring and, if necessary, keep rotating the range input. Everything else was done by the computer.

HIT OR MISS

Quite simply, the K-14 made the difference between missing the target and hitting it. Thousands of combat reports testify to this. For example, Capt. John B. England (357th FG): "I was travelling at approximately 400 miles per hour (643.6km/h) and made a very tight turn into him, and closed to about 500 yards. I placed him within my K-14 and squeezed the trigger. I got strikes all over the engine and cockpit. The enemy aircraft, burning and smoking excessively, crashed into a river . . . My wing man said I was pulling 6g when I got this Jerry."

Above: A beautiful design and a delight to fly, but the row of six Swastikas below the canopy testify to the P-51D's fighting abilities.

The P-51 D and K

SPECIFICATION

P-51D Mustang

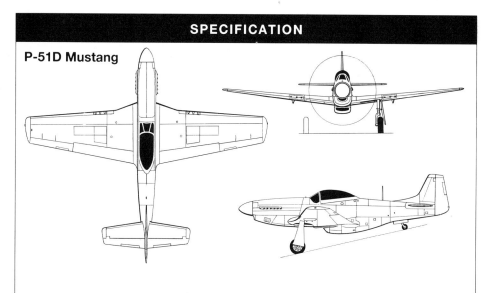

Dimensions
Length: 32ft 3in (9.84m)
Height: 13ft 8in (4.17m)
Wing span: 37ft 0½in (11.30m)
Gross wing area: 233sq ft (21.65m²)

Weights
Empty: 7,635lb (3,466kg)
Normal take-off: 10,100lb (4,585kg)
Maximum loaded: 12,100lb (5,493kg)

Power
1 × Packard V-1650–7 (licence-built Rolls-Royce Merlin 61 series) 12-cylinder liquid-cooled Vee piston engine rated at 1,490bhp at take-off, and 1,720bhp at War Emergency setting

Performance
Maximum speed: 437mph (703km/h) at 25,000ft (7,625m)
Initial rate of climb: 3,475ft/min (1,060m/min)
Service ceiling: 41,900ft (12,780m)
Combat range: 950 miles (1,526km)
Operational range: 1,650 miles (2,655km) with two drop tanks

In the European theatre of operations the P-51D/K not only did more than any other single type to destroy the Luftwaffe, but they carried out countless bombing and rocket-firing missions, and often found themselves in the Soviet Union, Romania, Yugoslavia and anywhere else that was too distant for other fighters. In flying these long missions, the pilot obviously needed a "relief tube", and many also took along a packet of sandwiches for nourishment. A further enormous help was a new kind of drop tank, designed by Pytram Ltd and produced in vast quantities by two British firms. Though it increased capacity to 90 US gal (340.6 litre), it was made from an early form of plastic based on formaldehyde-bonded lamina-tions of paper. Despite being popularly known as "the paper tank", it could hold on to 750lb (340.5kg) of petrol in 6g manoeuvres. Once used, it quickly deteriorated, and after being dropped it gave the enemy no usable raw material, as did other fuel tanks.

FAR EAST FORCE

In the Pacific theatre, the P-51D/K equipped the 15th and 21st FGs from March 1945, and the 506th FG from May, immediately proving themselves the most valuable AAF fighters in the region. RAF units wholly Mk IV/IVA-equipped were: Nos. 19, 26, 64, 65, 93, 112, 118, 122, 126, 129, 154, 165, 213, 234 and 611 Squadrons; Nos. 303, 306, 309, 315 and 316 (Polish) Squadrons; Nos. 441 and 442 (Canadian) Squadrons; No. 3 (Australian) Squadron; and No. 5 (South African) Squadron.

In the Pacific theatre, the RAAF had Spitfire VIIIs, but these had totally inadequate range. In 1944 a licence was obtained for production of the P-51D in Australia, with assembly by the Common-wealth Aircraft Corporation (CAC). To get things started, NAA supplied 100 sets of parts, and Packard supplied 80 V-1650-3 engines. The initial result was 80 CA-17 Mustang Mk XX fighters, the first flying on 29 April 1945. These were followed by 40 CA-18 Mustang 21s with the Dash-7 engine; 14 Mustang 22s with the RAF installation of an F24 oblique camera behind the cockpit; and 66 Mustang 23s with the British-built Merlin 66 or 70. A total of 14 Mk 21s was subsequently converted to Mk 22s. In addition, the RAAF received 214 P-51Ds and 84 P-51Ks on Lend-Lease, as well as one field transfer from the USAAF, but no RAAF Mustangs became operational until well after the end of the war, though they went on to do sterling work during the Korean War in the early 1950s.

Above: The majority of P-51D/Ks had the ability to carry up to four 5in (12.7cm) rocket projectiles on short underwing stub rails, as used by this Australian ground attack P-51D.

North American P-51 Mustang

Left: Armed and ready, a USAAF F-51D waits, its pilot looking for the signal to take off and make his way to another Communist target during the Korean War.

Below: During the 1960s, a handful of F-51Ds (foreground) and a single TF-51D (background) were converted by the Cavalier Co. as potentially low-cost ground attack aircraft.

One other wartime development deserves mention. In early-1943 the US Navy (USN) carried out an urgent study of the Mustang to see whether it could quickly be turned into a carrier-based fighter. At that time, no shipboard fighters were available except the Grumman F4F Wildcat, and the long range and high performance of the Mustang made it look very appealing. In May 1943 the Navy requested NAA to modify a P-51 for carrier trials. It was obvious that, in addition to the provision of a hook, many modifications would be needed. While these were being designed, company test pilot Bob Chilton flew a regular P-51D through a series of simulated deck landings. In fact, by the summer of 1943 the Grumman F6F Hellcat and Chance-Vought F4U Corsair had entered service, and pressure for a carrier-based P-51 all but evaporated. Thus it was not until 15 November 1944 that Lt. R. M. Elder, USN, made the first of a long series of arrested landings aboard

the USN escort carrier USS *Shangri-La* (CV-38). The aircraft incorporated 90 modifications, about 30 of them connected with the installation of the long sting-type arrester hook immediately behind the tail-wheel. It was not equipped or strengthened for catapult take-offs.

In 1948 the TP-51D was redesignated TF-51D. By this time, most either had no armament or just four 0.5in guns. One

aircraft was converted for shipboard landing tests. Like the original hooked Mustang, it had by this time been fitted with the taller vertical tail of the P-51H, as described in the next chapter.

Below: Taking the Cavalier concept a stage further, Piper developed the Enforcer in response to the USAF's Pave Coin programme.

Above: Following Bob Chilton's simulated deck landings, a TP-51D was modified for a series of actual deck landings. Here, Lt. R.M. Elder takes the wire on one such test.

BESSEMER PUBLIC LIBRARY

WHEREAS the RAF, and British technical staff, showed surprisingly little interest in "their" American fighter in 1940–41, by 1942 the scene had changed dramatically. So good was the Mustang that hordes of Ministry of Aircraft Production officials, technical staff at RAE Farnborough and RAF engineering personnel were showing an interest in almost every rivet. Among other things it was found that, having made allowances for various design differences, the airframe was heavier than that of the Spitfire V by a significant amount, though both were designed to the same load factors. Discussions with NAA in early-1943 revealed that the Inglewood design team were already considering a thorough redesign of the entire aircraft, mainly to reduce weight but also to simplify systems, improve maintenance, and enhance performance without changing the engine. It was agreed that this "second generation" Mustang should be designed to a combination of the optimum British and American strength requirements, but mainly as laid down in British Air Publication 970.

The work went ahead under charge number NA-105, five aircraft being authorized. Resemblance to previous Mustangs was almost coincidental, because as far as the structure was concerned no single part remained unaltered. A totally new aeroplane was designed on the proverbial clean sheet of paper, and many of the points of detail design were completely different, though the overall dimensions were kept very close to those of the highly successful P-51D.

The main landing gears were redesigned, partly because of the predicted reduced maximum weight of 11,500lb (5,221kg) and partly because, despite the obvious need to operate from rough front-line airstrips, the wheels and tyres were greatly reduced in size. Several writers have stated

Above: The first of the lightweight Mustangs was the XP-51F, three of which were built (one being sent to the United Kingdom). Among the more obvious features are the lengthened canopy and smaller landing gear.

that this enabled the wing leading-edge kink to be eliminated; it was indeed eliminated, but in fact the redesigned wing was actually larger, the leading-edge being a straight line from the original root to the tip, and the area increasing from 233 to 235sq ft. Purely to reduce weight, the inboard guns were deleted, the remaining four having 440 rounds each, the wing tanks were reduced in size to 102 US gal (386 litre) each and the fuselage tank was eliminated. One of the less obvious features was that the wing aerofoil was changed to an even newer low-drag "laminar flow" profile. Another was that each main leg pivoted in a dural forging instead of a large casting in magnesium alloy, the front spar now being straight.

Inside the redesigned fuselage were completely new structures and systems.

The engine mounting was simplified, the "integral" cradle saving over 100lb (45.4kg) in weight and improving access to items around the engine. The hydraulic system was greatly simplified and increased in pressure, operating jacks being reduced in size and the wheel brakes being of the new disc type. The coolant and intercooler radiators were again redesigned and installed in a completely new duct which, among other changes, had a vertical inlet standing even further away from the underside of the wing. One major improvement was to remove the oil cooler from the rear radiator group, enabling the latter to be made smaller and eliminating the long and vulnerable oil pipes. Instead, the oil was passed through a heat exchanger on the front of the oil tank and next to the engine intercooler, whose flow of glycol effectively carried away the heat from the oil.

The cockpit layout was improved with a simplified engine control box and a central arrangement of instruments similar to the British basic blind-flying panel. The pilot's back armour was made integral with the seat. The canopy was again re-designed, and though it was enormous – much bigger even than that of the P-51D – the drag was reduced. Though looking superficially similar, all control surfaces were improved, the tail surfaces all being larger (but at the same time lighter). Tabs were enlarged, the aileron trim tab being on the left surface only and right at its inboard end, and the ailerons were given a 15deg movement instead of 12deg. Chord of flaps and ailerons were made equal. Weight and cost were both saved by replacing many minor metal parts with moulded plastics, including both Bakelite-type phenolics and glassfibre.

LIGHTWEIGHT DEBUT

The first of the new lightweight Mustangs to be completed was one of three XP-51Fs, while the third aircraft, designated Mustang Mk V, was finished in RAF camouflage. Powerplant of the F-model was the same Packard V-1650-7 as used in all except the first P-51D/Ks, but more weight was saved by fitting an Aero-products Unimatic propeller with only three blades of the new edge-welded hollow

Below: Reflecting British interest and involvement in the development of lightweight Mustangs, the second XP-51G had RAF camouflage applied and was flight tested in the UK.

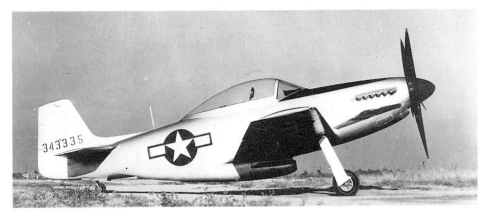

steel type. Bob Chilton made the first flight on 14 February 1944, and subsequent testing confirmed a level speed of 466mph (750km/h) at 29,000ft (8,845m). Equipped empty weight was just 2,000lb (908kg) less than that of the P-51D, 5,635lb (2,558kg) against 7,635lb (3,466kg). Combat gross weight was 9,060lb (4,113kg), roughly 1,600lb (726.4kg) below the corresponding figure for the P-51D. In England, the A&AEE at Boscombe Down found the Mustang Mk V to weigh only 7,855lb (3,580kg) in interceptor trim, and overall rated it very highly, except for a severe lack of directional stability which required frequent heavy applications by the pilot of rudder in some flight conditions.

The other two lightweights were completed as XP-51Gs, and though they

Above: Very similar to the XP-51F in many ways, the XP-51G differed primarily in having a completely new engine, namely the Rolls-Royce RM.14SM, and a five-bladed prop.

had Merlin engines, the powerplant could hardly have been more different. The whole package was supplied from Britain comprising a Merlin Mk 145 (company experimental designation RM.14SM), driving a Rotol propeller with five densi-fied-wood blades (almost identical to the propeller of the Spitfire XIV). Ed Virgin flew the first XP-51G on 10 August 1944, and it was immediately apparent that this was the "hottest ship" NAA had ever built. Combat weight was only 8,879lb (4,031kg), and level speed reached 485mph (780km/h) at 20,750ft (6,329m). The No. 2 aircraft was finished in British livery and also called a Mustang V, and it was widely reported to have reached 495mph (796.4km/h) during trials at the A&AEE in February 1945. The P-51F/Gs would have had provision for fuel tanks, bombs or ten rockets, but the attachments were not subsequently fitted.

Whether or not the XP-51G ever did nudge 500mph (804.5km/h) is a moot point, for the design was not taken any further. Not least of the problems was that the Merlin 100-series, of which the Mk 145 was an advanced member, were not quite ready for production. In any case, NAA needed engines from Packard, which

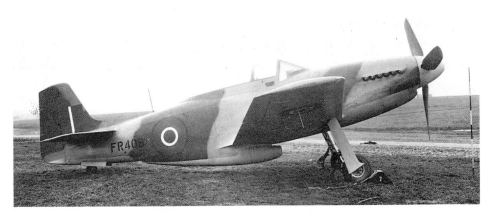

Lightweights and Exports

had set up its own development programme. Coming along behind the V-1650-7 was the Dash-9 engine, structurally strengthened and modified in minor details to enable it to have a war emergency power of 1,900hp at about 20,000ft (6,100m) with water/alcohol injection and 150-grade fuel. Packard said they could deliver the Dash-9 from late-1944, so it was chosen to power the next production Mustang. Under some pressure, NAA then designed the aircraft itself, the NA-126, which was ordered into production as the P-51H in June 1944 before much of it had even been drawn on paper.

As a basis NAA took the NA-105, which had proved to be an outstanding aircraft. The V-1650-9 was, however, geared to an Aeroproducts Unimatic propeller with four blades, though it was still lighter than the propeller with the same hub fitted to the P-51K. At the other end, the fin and rudder were significantly increased in height and the rear fuselage lengthened to an overall length of 33ft 4in (10.16m) which,

Above: Based on the XP-51F, the production-standard P-51H featured a lengthened fuselage. It was the only production version of the P-51 not to be used in active combat.

Below: This head-on view of a P-51H reveals three modifications that were incorporated in this model: the four-bladed propeller, smaller chin air scoop, and deeper radiator lip.

together with a dorsal fin which had been absent from the P-51F/G, at last cured the yawing instability that had never been far from all Mustangs from the P-51D onward. The cockpit hood was much shorter than that of the F, and almost identical in size to that on late D production, though the profile was quite different, the top of the hump being at the front. The fuselage was further modified to raise the cockpit to give an 8deg gunsight deflection angle looking down along the almost straight top line from gunsight to spinner. Armament returned to six guns, and access for servicing was improved by detail redesign of the wing doors and feed system, and by making the ammunition boxes removable. The fuselage fuel tank was also restored, though its capacity was fixed at 50 US gal (191 litres), giving a total internal capacity of 255 US gal (965 litres).

This was the ultimate production single-engined Mustang, and it was intended, with the P-47N, to be the leading AAF fighter in the campaign to defeat Japan.

Above: A taller tail fin was fitted to the majority of P-51Hs as they were built, and retrofitted to the early production aircraft. Note also the shorter teardrop canopy.

An order was placed for 2,000, made up of 555 NA-126 and 1,445 NA-129 with very minor differences. All these were to be built at Inglewood. A further 1,629 were ordered from Dallas as NA-124s, their AAF designation being P-51M. These differed chiefly in having the Dash-9A engine with a lower emergency rating caused by deletion of the water injection. To follow on from the P-51M, the Dallas plant was to build the most powerful of all the Mustangs, the NA-129, designated P-51L. This was essentially a P-51H fitted with the V-1650-11 engine and the Stromberg speed/density injection-type carburettor. (Note: this engine did not, as often reported, have direct fuel injection). At a manifold pressure of 90in (228.6cm) (almost 30lb [13.6kg] boost), the Dash-11 was rated at peak height at 2,270hp with water injection, the most powerful of all production models of the Rolls-Royce Merlin engine.

TALL TAIL

Bob Chilton flew the first P-51H on 3 February 1945. This aircraft, like the next 19, retained the P-51F tail, the distinctive tall unit being fitted on aircraft No. 21 and

being retrofitted to earlier aircraft. Gross weight was 9,500lb (4,313kg) clean, or up to 11,500lb (5,221kg) with maximum external stores. In clean condition, it established a level speed of 487mph (783.5km/h) at 25,000ft (7,625m), making it the fastest production aeroplane of the Second World War, apart from the German jets. A single H-1 was supplied to Britain for evaluation, becoming KN987. The 1,445 NA-129s were cancelled at the end of the war. A single P-51M-1-NT was built at Dallas, but the other 1,628 were cancelled. The impressive P-51L was the subject of an order for 1,700, but once again, the whole contract was cancelled before any were completed due to the end of hostilities.

Last of all the single-engined Mustangs was yet another in the NA-105 family of lightweights. Designated XP-51J, two examples were ordered. Though having almost exactly the same wings, cockpit, tail and landing gear as the XP-51F, the XP-51J had a substantially modified fuselage resulting from the fact that the engine reverted to the Allison V-1710. It was, however, the Dash-119 version of the engine, a totally different animal from the F3R and Dash-39. With two-stage, gear-driven superchargers, it was rated at 1,500hp for take-off and, with water/alcohol injection, 1,720hp at 20,700ft (6,313m). Whereas the P-51F/G were fractionally shorter than the P-51D/K at 32ft 2.7in (9.83m), the XP-51J had a length of 32ft 11in (10.04m). It was also heavier, at 6,030lb (2,737kg) empty. Unlike earlier V-1710s the engine had an updraught carburettor, but there were no inlets around the nose at all. Instead, the carburettor air was taken in through a ram inlet at the front of the radiator duct, and thence

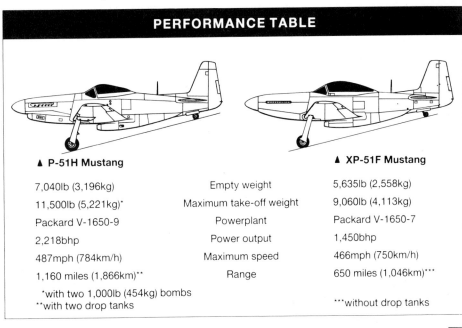

PERFORMANCE TABLE

▲ P-51H Mustang		▲ XP-51F Mustang
7,040lb (3,196kg)	Empty weight	5,635lb (2,558kg)
11,500lb (5,221kg)*	Maximum take-off weight	9,060lb (4,113kg)
Packard V-1650-9	Powerplant	Packard V-1650-7
2,218bhp	Power output	1,450bhp
487mph (784km/h)	Maximum speed	466mph (750km/h)
1,160 miles (1,866km)**	Range	650 miles (1,046km)***

*with two 1,000lb (454kg) bombs
**with two drop tanks

***without drop tanks

Lightweights and Exports

Above: In addition to receiving P-51Ds built under licence by CAC, the Royal Australian Air Force was the recipient of no less than 298 Lend-Lease P-51Ds from the USA.

piped to the engine. Some development was needed to make this pipe compact yet efficient.

By the time the XP-51J came along, the war was clearly in its final stages, and there was a perceptible easing of pressure. Nevertheless, the aircraft was put through a brief flight-test programme, the first flight being made by Joe Barton on 23 April 1945. Maximum speed had been calculated at an impressive 491mph (790km/h) at 27,400ft (8,357m), but the engine was not yet cleared for full-power operation and no performance measurements were possible. The No. 2 aircraft was never flown, but was shipped to Allison for use as a source of spare parts.

EXPORT SUCCESS

Total production of all single-engined Mustangs amounted to 15,575 in the USA and 100 (discounting aircraft assembled from US parts) in Australia. Mustangs, mainly of the B/C/D/K models, were credited with 4,950 of the 10,720 victories in air combat claimed by the USAAF in Europe, and 4,131 of the 8,160 ground-straffing claims in the same theatre of operations. At the end of the war, the USAAF had some 5,500 P-51s and F-6s.

Above: The Royal Canadian Air Force was one of many post-war P-51 users. This example served with No.420 "City of Winnipeg" Squadron.

Below: A total of 95 P-51Ds was supplied to the South African Air Force, these seeing active combat during the Korean War.

PRODUCTION

P-51D Production

AAF Serials:
44-13253 – 44-14052
44-14053 – 44-14852
44-14853 – 44-15252
44-15253 – 44-15752
44-63160 – 44-64159
44-72027 – 44-72126
44-72127 – 44-72626
44-72627 – 44-73626
44-73627 – 44-74226
44-74227 – 44-75026
44-11153 – 44-11352
44-84390 – 44-84989
45-11343 – 45-11542
45-11543 – 45-11742

TP-51D Production

AAF Serials:
45-11443 – 45-11450
44-84610 – 44-84611
44-13918

Above: Both Nationalist (Taiwan) and the People's Republic of China acquired examples of war-surplus **Mustangs. Illustrated is a P-51D bearing the insignia of the Air Force of the People's Liberation Army.**

Above: Large numbers of ex-USAF F-51Ds were withdrawn from storage and hastily supplied to the Republic **of Korea Air Force (ROKAF) as the Korean War escalated. They were to be used in the ground attack role.**

the RAF and Commonwealth air forces approximately 1,480, the Free French air force about 100, the Swedish Flygvapnet (air force) 50 (plus four ex-USAAF examples which force-landed in Sweden), the Chinese Nationalists 50 and the Soviet Union a very small number (which were never in front-line service). Deliveries to Italy were just beginning, and subsequently Mustangs, almost all of them ex-USAAF P-51Ds or P-51Ks, served with the air forces of at least 26 countries, including: Australia, Bolivia, Canada, China (Nationalist and the People's Republic), Cuba, Dominica, France, Guatemala, Haiti, Honduras, Indonesia, Israel, Italy, Netherlands (and N. East Indies), Nicaragua, New Zealand, Philippines, Salvador, Somalia, South Africa, South Korea, Sweden, Switzerland, United Kingdom and Uruguay.

NEW DESIGNATIONS

Of course, despite the rapid run-down of wartime units and the replacement of piston-engined fighters by jets, the USAAF P-51 force remained considerable for many years. The AAF became the United States Air Force (USAF) in 1947, and a year later the P-51 was redesignated F-51. Other designation changes included: F-6D to FP-51D; TP-51D to TF-51D; and two-seat F-6D conversions became TRF-51D. Using post-1948 designations, while the USAF F-51D/K force quickly dwindled, almost all the new F-51H production examples took their place, and proved very successful. In May 1946, the Air National Guard (ANG) was re-formed, and ANG fighter units received virtually all of the F-51D/K Mustangs withdrawn from regular USAF service. In December 1948, these aircraft numbered over 700 and equipped 28 ANG squadrons. The force continued to grow, soon adding squadrons of RF-51Ds, and in the Korean War (1950–53), no fewer than 22 of the 27 ANG wings saw front-line service. During that conflict the USAF began to retire its F-51Hs, and by 1952 no fewer than 68 of the 98 ANG squadrons were flying Mustangs, mainly F-51D/Hs. These well-liked aircraft were progressively replaced by jets, and the final US Mustang mission was a ferry flight by the last F-51D (44-72948) of the 167th FS from West Virginia ANG headquarters at Charleston to the Air Force Museum at Wright-Patterson AFB, Ohio, where "948" now has a well-earned place of honour.

Below: Mustangs were to equip many Air National Guard units in the post-war years. One such operator was the Indiana ANG, whose Mustang force included a number of TF-51D two-seat conversion trainers.

THE Twin Mustang is one of those brilliant ideas that one wishes had been thought of earlier. Like the British de Havilland Hornet, it was a long-range fighter which could have been designed back in 1940, and could have played a valuable part in the Second World War, but instead missed the war altogether. In the case of the Twin Mustang, this was because back in 1940 the need for such an aircraft was simply not there.

It was not until 1943 that such aircraft as the P-38 Lightning and even the Mustang itself were assigned combat missions lasting anything up to seven hours. These proved to be a severe strain on the pilots, who returned not only drenched in perspiration, but so exhausted that they sometimes had to be lifted from the cockpit. It seemed obvious that there was an urgent need for a superior long-range escort fighter accommodating two pilots, who could take turns in flying the aircraft. None of the special-purpose escorts had two pilots, and in any case, the P-51 with a rear-fuselage fuel tank had shown itself dramatically better than any of them. There was a two-seater, the Lockheed XP-58, but this large and un-gainly machine had a pilot and a gunner, which did nothing to solve the problem.

In November 1943 NAA made a formal proposal for what was naturally called the Twin Mustang. The idea was that two Mustangs should be joined together by a common wing centre section and tail-plane, as had been done with several pre-vious wartime aircraft. Seldom has a proposal been better received, nor moved faster. The AAF assigned the designation XP-82, and on 7 January 1944 ordered four prototypes. NAA assigned the desig-nation NA-120. At an early stage it was noticed that, once the war was over, Packard would be most unlikely to con-

Above: Originally proposed as a long-range escort fighter to accompany US bombers on raids against targets in Japan, the Twin Mustang was just too late to see any action during the Second World War.

tinue to build V-1650 Merlin engines, and moreover that the Allison V-1710 had matured into an engine which, without a turbo-supercharger, but with two stages of gear-driven blowers, could give excel-lent performance at all altitudes (it was for this reason that the V-1710-119 was later selected for the XP-51J). Thus, the third and fourth prototypes were specified to have the V-1710-119, and were desig-nated XP-82A. The basic airframe was to be based on the P-51H.

Of course, from the start the NAA designers knew it was going to be a big job. Each change inevitably has a knock-on effect, triggering a chain reaction which often threatens to leave nothing unaltered. The easy parts were adding the new wing centre section, with a full-span slotted flap, and a rectangular tailplane and tabbed elevator. That was just the beginning. To guarantee good yaw stab-ility, the rear fuselages were lengthened by no less than 57in (145cm), mainly aft of the radiator group, and the dorsal fins were greatly enlarged. Oddly, the first two XP-82s had vertical tails almost iden-tical to that of the P-51D, not the P-51H as in all subsequent Twin Mustangs.

NAA carefully studied the simple solu-tion of modifying the landing gear as little as possible. Obviously some changes had to be made, if only to shorten the two inboard units, hinged near the centreline, to take account of the fact that the centre

Above: The XP-82s made use of the fuselages from XP-51Fs, these being joined by a completely new wing centre section and single-piece horizontal tailplane.

wing was horizontal, thus bringing the hinges nearer the ground. After much argument, it was decided to start afresh and design an optimized two-unit main landing gear. This came out considerably shorter than the P-51 gear, though with stronger legs, larger multi-ply tyres and high-capacity disc brakes in order for each wheel to handle (in production versions) twice the weight of a fully loaded P-51. Each unit was configured to retract inwards hydraulically, lying with the leg enclosed by a curved door in the underside of the adjacent fuselage, and the wheel on the far side in the centre section. Cables from the main gear pulled up the steerable/castoring tailwheels, each of which was fitted with a twin-tread tyre to avoid any shimmy on landing.

All parts of the wing were completely redesigned internally, partly to carry manoeuvring loads at the very much greater gross weight. While maximum weight was to be doubled, from approximately 12,000 to 24,000lb (5,448 to 10,896kg), wing area was increased by

only 78 per cent, resulting in an appreciable rise in wing loading and structural stresses. Another reason for redesign was that fuel capacity was greatly increased. Four self-sealing wing tanks were provided, with a total of 574 US gal (2,180 litre). Each outer wing contained a cell of 196 US gal (741 litre) capacity, and each inner wing (under the fuselage and extending just into the centre section) had a tank of 91 US gal (344.5 litre). Yet a further reason for redesign was that the wing leading-edge was, in later versions, equipped for thermal de-icing, as also were the leading edges of the fins and tailplane.

Hot air was piped from a heater and blower unit in each rear fuselage, this being fed with warm air passed on from the radiator duct.

Basic armament comprised six MG53-2 guns, as in later P-51s, but with the difference that each gun had 440 rounds of ammunition. All six were grouped in the middle of the centre section, fed from

Below: An impressive array of guns, bombs and rockets could be carried by the Twin Mustang. The six guns carried in the wing centre section were augmented by an eight-gun pod.

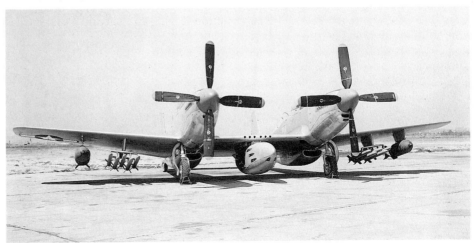

Double Trouble

ammunition boxes occupying the entire space behind the main spar as far as the inner fuel tanks. The centre section was stressed to carry heavy external loads on either one or two pylons, with individual weights up to the 2,100lb (953kg) of the new 310 US gal (1,173 litre) drop tank. The outer wings were likewise stressed for two pylons with similar loads. The gunsight was to be the K-18, an improved US version of the K-14.

DOUBLE COCKPITS

Most systems were based on those of the P-51H, though there were detail differences (for example, the oxygen bottles were larger, reflecting the greater flight endurance). The cockpits, however, were not identical, nor the same as each other. That in the left fuselage was complete, and from the start was also fitted with controls for a simple three-axis autopilot, the right cockpit merely having an emergency autopilot disengage switch. Everything was arranged so that the left pilot could be in command, while the right-hand pilot could take over intermittently, and land the aircraft in emergency. Both cockpits had their own heating and oxygen supplies, and both sets of rudder pedals could, if necessary, be disconnected and stowed. The left cockpit contained the D/F loop antenna behind the pilot's head armour (in prototypes it was above the rear fuselage), while the HF radio mast was positioned above the right-hand rear fuselage.

Small changes were also made to the flight control system. In some early aircraft, the elevator had two tabs, one at each end, while in later aircraft, both spring and trim tabs were grouped at the centre. The rudders differed only in detail from those of the P-51H, but the ailerons were markedly different. Because of the greater rolling inertia of the twinned aircraft, each aileron was increased in length, retaining the full 15deg movement introduced with the P-51H, and then divided into inner and outer sections

to prevent binding of the hinges under high g loads. The lateral control system was then boosted by an hydraulic cylinder in the right-hand fuselage, as the Twin Mustang always tended to roll about the left-hand fuselage.

The further NAA got with the design, the more exciting the P-82 looked, and it was soon clear that it would be a real winner, combining similar fighting qualities of the P-51 with the range and endurance needed to escort Boeing B-29 Superfortress long-range bombers all the way to Japan. In late 1944, long before an XP-82 had flown, the USAAF placed an order for 500 production P-82Bs. The first example took to the air on its maiden flight on 15 April 1945, but by this time

Below: An impressive machine both on the ground and in the air, the Twin Mustang possessed excellent performance capabilities. However, production was to be limited.

the decision had been taken, in view of the apparently imminent end to the war, to confine the whole programme to NAA's Inglewood plant, operations at Dallas being run down and, after war's end, terminated. The XP-82s were unpainted except for black anti-dazzle panels, just like the NA-73X some five years earlier. Both were powered by Packard V-1650-23/25 engines, driving four-blade Aeroproducts propellers of P-51H type (except that the Dash-25 engine in the left fuselage was handed, with left-hand rotation, requiring a "mirror image" propeller). Combat weight was 19,100lb (8,671kg), and level speed 482mph (775.5km/h) at 25,100ft (7,655m). The range on internal fuel was 1,390 miles (2,236km).

With such performance, the AAF was almost sorry the war was coming to an end! The order for 500 production aircraft had been intended as just the first batch, but no less than 480 of these were subsequently cancelled. Designated P-82B,

the 20 survivors differed only in detail from the prototypes, the engines being a V-1650-9 (a standard P-51H unit) and, in the left fuselage, a V-1650-21 with left-hand rotation. The 20 P-82Bs never saw active service, though they followed the P-51H on the Inglewood production line in November 1945. Instead, 12 were used for training and the other eight for tests of every conceivable kind of external store, not least being a centreline pod housing a row of eight 0.5in machine-guns and their ammunition.

The tenth aircraft was converted in 1946 into an experimental night fighter designated XP-82C. A huge pod slung under the centreline housed all the radar equipment, apart from the controls and display which were in the right cockpit, whose occupant became the radar operator. The radar was the SCR-720, the most important US interception radar of the period, and which was then being used by Northrop P-61 Black Widow night fighters. In this radar the antenna spun continuously at high speed about a vertical axis, transmitting and receiving about a large sector ahead. To avoid interference from the propellers it was necessary to position the antenna ahead of them, and this meant that the entire pod had to be cantilevered ahead of the pylon, placing severe nodding loads on the pod, pylon and wing. Much work had to be done to avoid distortion, because movement of the radar axis relative to the aircraft would result in false indications of target direction.

SMALLER RADAR

The 11th P-82B was similarly converted into the XP-82D. This experimental night fighter was similar to the XP-82C model, except that it had a different radar. The APS-4 was a much smaller set, operating in the 1.1in (3cm) waveband, which meant that the scanning antenna could be much smaller. The power unit, transmitter and receiver were also smaller. By 1946 it seemed probable that the Twin

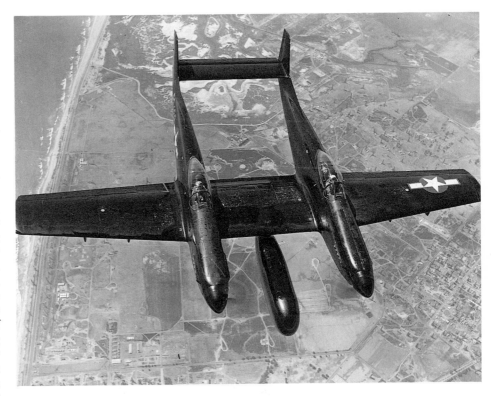

Above: Looking sinister in its overall black night fighter finish, this was the sole XP-82D produced. The prominent centre pod housed an APS-4 search radar unit.

Mustang would find employment mainly as a night fighter, because it could do everything a P-61 could do and do it better and faster. Northrop's XP-89 purpose-designed jet night fighter was years away from service.

As predicted, the end of the war saw production of Packard V-1650 Merlin engines come to an end. One of the two XP-82A prototypes was cancelled, but the other was completed and flown (contrary to what is often claimed). The engines were both Allison V-1710-119s, both turning 11ft (3.35m) Aeroproducts four-blade propellers in the same (right-hand) direction. The installation now looked not unlike a Merlin, because the Dash-119 had an updraught inlet and

injection-type carburettor upstream of the two superchargers, so the inlet was on the underside behind the spinner. The inlet was about 1ft (0.30m) further back than with the Merlin, and there were many other differences. The oil was once more cooled by an air radiator upstream of the main glycol radiator, as in the P-51D, and a 14.4 US gal (54.5 litre) water/alcohol injection tank was located beneath each engine. The flight-test programme with the XP-82A paved the way for future P-82s to have the Allison engine, and the powerplant selected was the V-1710-143/145. As the designation indicates, these engines were handed, as in the XP-82: the Dash-143 in the left fuselage had left-hand rotation, and the Dash-145 on the right side was right-handed – in other words, the propeller blades moved apart at the top. Quite unlike early V-1710s, these engines were cleared to 3,200rpm for take-off (even higher than a Merlin) at which the rating

Double Trouble

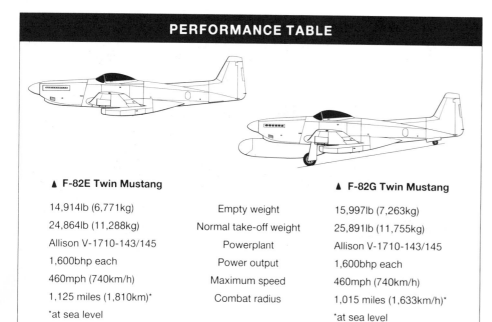

PERFORMANCE TABLE

F-82E Twin Mustang		F-82G Twin Mustang
14,914lb (6,771kg)	Empty weight	15,997lb (7,263kg)
24,864lb (11,288kg)	Normal take-off weight	25,891lb (11,755kg)
Allison V-1710-143/145	Powerplant	Allison V-1710-143/145
1,600bhp each	Power output	1,600bhp each
460mph (740km/h)	Maximum speed	460mph (740km/h)
1,125 miles (1,810km)*	Combat radius	1,015 miles (1,633km)*
*at sea level		*at sea level

While the P-82E was in production, on 27/28 February 1947, a P-82B (44-65168) flew at maximum continuous power from Hawaii to New York, averaging 342mph (550km/h) for 5,051 miles (8,127km), by far the longest non-stop flight by a piston-engined fighter.

Before delivery, nine F-82Fs and five F-82Gs (46-384/388) were winterized for service with the 449th All-Weather (AW) Sqn at Ladd AFB, Alaska. This left 91 F-82Fs, fitted with the simple APG-28 tracking radar, but with extremely good night and bad-weather avionics. The aircraft were painted all-black, and had flame-damped exhausts which, plus the drag of

Below: Proof of the Twin Mustang's impressive endurance and range was provided by "Betty Jo", an F-82B which flew non-stop from Hawaii to New York in some 15 hours.

was 1,600hp. Maximum with water/alcohol was 1,930hp at sea level and 1,700 hp at 21,000ft (6,405m) giving a performance very similar to that of an aircraft fitted with Merlins.

Having got the Allison matched to the airframe, the AAF's first peacetime budget, in 1946, despite being tiny by wartime standards, did contain funding for 250 Twin Mustangs. These comprised: 100 P-82E day fighter-bombers; 100 P-82F night fighters; and 50 P-82G night fighters. These completed Twin Mustang production. The aircraft's service designation was changed to F-82 in 1948.

ESCORT SERVICE

Of course, being the simplest, the F-82E was the first to enter service, reaching the 27th Fighter Escort Wing (FEW) of USAF Strategic Air Command (SAC) in 1948. Though having great weapons capability, they spent their brief life carrying fuel tanks and flying alongside B-29s, in the course of which it was discovered that if you were on the left of a formation, then the right-hand pilot did the flying.

Above: Seconds away from touchdown, this is one of a small number of F-82Fs which were "winterized" to facilitate operations in the frozen climes of Alaska. Several F-82Gs received the same treatment.

Above: Based much further south, in the state of Washington, the 318th F(AW)S flew from McChord AFB. In this view of one of the F-82Gs in service with the squadron, note how the radar pod extends ahead of the propeller disc into smoother air.

the radar pod, cut speed to about 459mph (738.5km/h). One slight problem was that, as the powerful landing lights were on the landing gears, directly behind the propellers, their use at night blinded the pilot, who thus had to land on taxi-lights only. The F-82F served with the 325th FG at both Hamilton Field, California, and McChord AFB, Washington, on the West Coast, and with the 52nd FG at Mitchel AFB and McGuire AFB, New Jersey, on the East Coast. The F-82G, like the F-82H, had the big SCR-720C radar, which, with just two fuel tanks, took the take-off weight to 26,208lb (11,898kg). Also painted overall black, these aircraft served with units based in the Pacific, initially with the 347th FG.

When the Korean War started on 25 June 1950, the 347th FG had two squadrons in Japan and one on Okinawa. Within 24 hours, all were operating from Itazuke AB, from where they had the range to reach the whole Korean peninsula. On 27 June F-82Gs of the 347th shot down a Lavochkin La-7, a Yakovlev Yak-9 and a Yak-11, to claim the first "kills" of

the war. Subsequently, the F-82s flew by day and night, but almost entirely in attack missions – and they were good at those too. The Korean War eventually ended in 1953; the same year that an F-82G flew the final Twin Mustang mission from the 449th (AW) Squadron's base at Ladd AFB, Alaska.

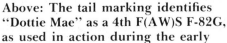

Above: The tail marking identifies "Dottie Mae" as a 4th F(AW)S F-82G, as used in action during the early days of the Korean War. The Twin Mustang would account for the first "kills" of the war in June 1950.

PRODUCTION

Twin Mustang Production

XP-82:	44-83886 – 44-83887
XP-82A:	44-83888
P-82B:	44-65160 – 44-65179
P-82C:	44-65169
P-82D:	44-65170
P-82E:	46-255 – 46-354
P-82F:	46-405 – 46-504
P-82G:	46-355 – 46-404
P-82H:	46-496 – 46-504
	46-384 – 46-388

Redesignations:
XP-82 to ZXF-82
P-82B to F-82B
P-82C to ZF-82C
P-82D to EF-82D
P-82E to F-82E
P-82F to F-82F
P-82G to F-82G
P-82H to F-82H

BESSEMER PUBLIC LIBRARY

INDEX

Page numbers in **bold** type refer to subjects mentioned in captions to illustrations.